Sprouts

SPROUTS

To Grow and Eat

Esther Munroe

THE STEPHEN GREENE PRESS

BRATTLEBORO, VERMONT

PUBLISHED DECEMBER 1974
Second printing December 1977—20,000 books in print

This book has been produced in the United States of America. It is composed by Priscilla Richardson and is published by The Stephen Greene Press, Brattleboro, Vermont, 05301.

The photographs for this book are by Allan Seymour.

Munroe, Esther, 1923–
    Sprouts to grow and eat.
    Includes index.
    1. Cookery (Sprouts) I. Title.
TX801.M87   641.6'3   74-23609
ISBN 0-8289-0226-7

Contents

PRACTICAL METRIC CONVERSIONS

Volume (workable approximates)

Teaspoon, **tsp**; tablespoon, **T**; fluid ounce, **fl.oz**; pint, **pt**; quart, **qt**; gallon, **gal** (all non-metric forms = established U.S.A. and Canadian measures); milliliter, **ml**; cubic centimeter, **cc** (1 **ml** = 1 **cc**); liter, **l**.

¼ tsp = 1.25 ml	4 cups (32 fl.oz/1 qt) = 950 ml/0.95 l.
½ tsp = 2.5 ml	2 qt = 1.90 l.
1 tsp = 5 ml	3 qt = 2.85 l.
1 T (½ fl.oz) = 15 ml	4 qt (1 gal) = 3.8 l.
2 T (1 fl.oz) = 30 ml	* * *
¼ cup (2 fl.oz) = 60 ml	100 ml = 3.4 fl.oz
1/3 cup (2.7 fl.oz) = 80 ml	500 ml = 17 fl.oz
½ cup (4 fl.oz) = 120 ml	1 l. = 1.06 qt
1 cup (8 fl.oz) = 240 ml/0.24 l.	1.5 l. = 1.59 qt
1½ cups (12 fl.oz) = 360 ml/0.36 l.	2 l. = 2.12 qt
2 cups (16 fl.oz/1 pt) = 470 ml/0.47 l.	5 l. = 1.30 gal

Weight/Mass (workable approximates)

Ounce avoirdupois, **oz.av**; gram, **g.**; pound, **lb**; kilogram (1,000 **g.**), **kg.**

½ oz.av = 14 g.	5 lb = 2.27 kg
1 oz.av = 28 g.	10 lb = 4.54 kg
4 oz.av (¼ lb) = 113 g.	* * *
8 oz.av (½ lb) = 226 g.	100 g. = 3.5 oz.av
12 oz.av (¾ lb) = 340 g.	1,000 g./1 kg = 2.2 lb
16 oz.av (1 lb) = 454 g./0.454 kg	2 kg = 4.4 lb
1½ lb = 680 g./0.680 kg	5 kg = 11.02 lb
2 lb = 908 g./0.908 kg	10 kg = 22.04 lb

Temperature

Fahrenheit, **F.**; Celsius (Centigrade), **C.** (rounded to nearest digit).

F.	C.	F.	C.	F.	C.	F.	C.	F.	C.
0	−18	80	27	195	91	275	135	425	218
10	−12	100	38	205	96	300	149	450	232
20	−7	145	63	212	100	325	163	475	246
32	0	165	74	220	104	350	177	500	260
40	4	185	85	238	114	375	191	525	274
50	10	190	88	240	116	400	204	550	288

Sprouts: A Food Bargain

Nearly three-quarters of the world's food supply comes from some form of seed: the grains (rice, corn, wheat, barley, rye, millet), or the legume family (beans, peas, lentils). The Old Testament of the Bible and other literatures of early people are full of references to these foodstuffs. So important were they to many cultures that the spirit of the seed was worshiped as a deity. The North American Indians reverenced the corn god as the giver of life. The fact that seeds could be transported readily and remain viable for long periods of time was one of the central reasons that people from one part of the world could migrate to another successfully.

A seed is essentially a plant in arrested development; that is to say, the seed must contain the potential for becoming a plant, and it must also contain those elements which are necessary to sustain it until the plant grows enough to be able to convert sunlight, water and soil nutrients into food. It is this duality in seeds that has caused them to be held in almost mystical awe and reverence. It is also this combination of elements that makes seeds such a valuable item of food for human beings and animals.

Throughout much of the world, seeds are eaten directly as a primary source of food. In other areas the tendency has been increasingly to feed seeds to livestock, which then become food for people. However, statistics published by the United States government show that an enormous amount of food value is lost when seeds are fed to animals first. For example, used as direct human food, one acre of wheat supplies 13 times as much protein, 17 times as many vitamins and 27 times as many calories as will the meat from beef that has been fed on that same acre of wheat. And, to put it in another way, an additional ten to thirty million people could be fed in the United States if the

1

present population exchanged one-third of its meat product intake for seeds.

As the world's population increases, the need for more foodstuffs also increases. To help meet this problem, it is already apparent to many authorities that more seeds will have to be used in some form for human food. Since 3000 B.C. the Chinese have recognized that sprouted seeds provide greater nutrition than just seeds alone. Sprouted rice, bean and pea seeds have played an important role in the Chinese diet. Several centuries ago the Russians started adding sprouted wheat to their black bread, recognizing that this gave them greatly increased nutrition, particularly, as we now know, Vitamin C.

Nutritional Advantages

It is really only in the past thirty years that we here in the Western hemisphere have become interested in sprouts and sprouting. During World War II considerable interest in sprouts was sparked in the United States by an article written by Dr. Clive M. McKay, Professor of Nutrition at Cornell University. Dr. McKay led off with this dramatic announcement: "Wanted! A vegetable that will grow in any climate, will rival meat in nutritive value, will mature in 3 to 5 days, may be planted any day of the year, will require neither soil nor sunshine, will rival tomatoes in Vitamin C, will be free of waste in preparation and can be cooked with as little fuel and as quickly as a . . . chop."

Dr. McKay was talking about soybean sprouts. He and a team of nutritionists had spent years researching the amazing properties of sprouted soybeans. They and other researchers at the universities of Pennsylvania and Minnesota, Yale and McGill have found that sprouts retain the B-complex vitamins present in the original seed, and show a big jump in Vitamin A and an almost unbelievable amount of Vitamin C over that present in unsprouted seeds. While some nutritionists point out that this high vitamin content is gained at the expense of some protein loss, the figures are impressive: an average 300 percent increase in Vitamin A and a 500 to 600 percent increase in Vitamin C. As a result, one-half cup of almost any sprouted seed provides as much Vitamin C as six glasses of orange juice. In addition, in the sprouting process starches are converted to simple sugars, thus making sprouts easily digested.

Other Advantages

There are many advantages beyond the nutritional advantages to be gained from using sprouts in the family diet.

Sprouts can be grown just about anywhere. All that is required are seeds, very simple equipment and small amounts of water.

The yield of sprouts to original seed is about 4 to 1; for example, 1 cup of wheat will make about 1 quart of wheat sprouts. This makes storage of enough seed for a large and varied sprout harvest possible in limited space.

Sprouts can be used in place of, or in conjunction with, other fresh vegetables, thus providing appetizing top-quality, garden-fresh vegetables when the market variety are either inferior in quality or very expensive. It should be pointed out that seeds for sprouting are not cheap (*they must be untreated by the various chemicals that many seed producers use and certified edible*); yet no foodstuff is cheap any longer and the cost of seeds for sprouting is still very low in relation to the edible yield.

Not the least of the advantages to incorporating sprouts in the diet is that they add a wonderful variety of textures and flavors.

Warning—only chemically untreated and certified edible seeds should be used for sprouting.

The Wonderful Variety

Most people are familiar with the mung bean sprouts that are used in Chinese food, but many have never heard about sprouting any other kind of seed. They ask, "Do they all taste alike?" The answer is that they don't taste any more alike than the different plants from which they derive.

Seeds from almost every vegetable commonly grown in North America can be sprouted and used for human food with great nutritional advantage. There are two common vegetables that do not produce edible sprouts: *tomato and potato sprouts are highly poisonous and should never be eaten.*

Wheat and rice sprouts have a sweet nut-like flavor; alfalfa, rye and clover sprouts have a fresh-green taste not unlike that of other salad greens; radish and mustard sprouts are somewhat peppery and should be used in conjunction with more bland foods; sprouts from seeds of the cabbage family—broccoli, Brussels sprouts, cauliflower and cabbage itself—taste rather like the parent plants; sprouts from each one of the many kinds of peas, beans and lentils have their own distinctive tastes and are particularly versatile in cooking.

For greatest food value, all of the edible sprouts may be eaten raw. All may also be cooked in many different ways, which are covered in the recipe section of this book. If sprouts are new to you and your family, it is suggested that you try several different kinds, both raw and cooked. You are certain to find some, and perhaps many, that you enjoy.

Anyone who likes vegetables—either raw or cooked—will find a whole new world of taste treats in sprouts. If you are careful not to mention the "this is good for you" aspect, most children will also like many sprouts.

Warning—only chemically untreated and certified edible seeds should be used for sprouting.

Getting Your Seeds

As mentioned earlier and as most home gardeners are already well aware, by far and away the largest percentage of seeds sold for planting have been treated with some chemical or other—the list is long and constantly changing. These chemicals are chiefly pesticides used to protect the seeds from various infestations. However, in some cases, for instance alfalfa and red clover, methyl dyes are used to indicate foreign origin. The latter, and many of the former, are highly toxic to human beings and, to make matters worse, accurate warnings are not always required to appear on the packaging. As a result, for safety's sake, *sprouts from seeds that have been treated with any chemical whatsoever have to be considered not fit for human consumption.*

One way to get seeds for sprouting is through the mail. A number of mail-order seed companies do sell a selection of untreated seeds. At the end of this book there is a partial list of such suppliers. However, to be on the safe side, always specify when ordering that you want only untreated seeds—seeds completely free of chemicals, and certified edible. And be sure to double check when your seeds arrive. This is more than worth the little effort involved.

Since more people have become interested in natural and/or untreated foods, many health food stores have begun to stock untreated seeds that are suitable for sprouting. If there is no natural food store available in your area, you may wish to consult the list of suppliers at the back of the book for the names of health food supply houses from whom you can order by mail. Once again, be sure to specify that you want untreated, edible seeds suitable for sprouting.

Most stores that specialize in Oriental foods also sell seeds for sprouting—particularly mung bean and soybeans, both of which are widely used in Far Eastern dishes.

In addition, many chain stores and supermarkets, as well as the corner market, sell brown rice, whole peas, beans and lentils of various kinds that are perfectly safe for sprouting. These seeds can sometimes be used successfully, although they are often not as satisfactory as those intended primarily for sprouting. They may well contain among them cracked or broken or too-old seeds that will not sprout. However, it is worth a try, especially if you can find a small store that doesn't treat its stock too roughly.

Anyone who lives in a rural area may be able to get some untreated seeds from the local grain dealer. Here again it is essential to be sure that the seeds are suitable for *human* consumption.

For the home gardener there is yet another alternative. Even though you cannot eat treated seeds, it is possible to plant those seeds to grow a crop of your own seeds that are safe to eat. Just select a few plants that seem particularly suitable and allow them to go to seed. Use no chemicals on the plants. Pick the seeds when they are fully mature, dry them completely and store in closed containers in a cool, dry, dark place. You then have your own untreated, fully wholesome seeds for sprouting—at almost no cost.

Warning—only chemically untreated and certified edible seeds should be used for sprouting.

Which Sprouts for What

Before going into the particulars about each sprout, there are a few generalities to bear in mind. Sprouts are always tastiest when young and fresh (in fact, they should rarely be allowed to reach over 1 inch in length). So it is best to sprout only a limited number of each variety at a time and to try to plan to have one crop eaten before the next harvest is ready.

Following is an alphabetical listing of the most commonly sprouted seeds, offering in a nutshell the specifics of recommended sprout length and sprouting time, plus general suggestions for use, for each sprout. Also see the "quick reference" table placed for convenience just before the recipe section. This table gives seed quantities and their expected sprout yield, plus handy information on growing and cooking (if any) times.

Once again, it is important to remember that the sprouting times given here are average times and may vary with the age of the seed, its moisture content and with the humidity and room temperature (some people feel that even the content of the water used affects the sprouting process). As a result, do not be bound by the exact times listed but rather by the length of the sprouts, being sure to harvest them before they pass their peak.

ADZUKI BEAN. These tiny red-brown beans are not as well known in the Western world as they deserve to be. In the Orient they have been grown for centuries and are often used in dishes for festive occasions. Easy to sprout, they are ready to eat in 4 or 5 days, at a sprouted length of ½ to 1 inch. Use adzuki bean sprouts in any recipe that calls for mung bean, soybean or any other legume sprouts.

ALFALFA. The name for this forage crop is Arabic, meaning "a fine, green fodder" and it derives from the fact that the Arabs discovered their horses grew stronger and more fleet on this crop than on any other. Sprouted for only 1 or 2 days, to a sprout length of 1/8 inch, alfalfa sprouts are particularly good in pastries, cereals and appetizers. If the sprouts are grown 4 or 5 days to about 1 inch and exposed to sunlight for a few hours, which allows them to develop chlorophyll, they make a delicious addition to fresh green salads. Alfalfa is one of the easiest of all seeds to sprout and, while the seed is fairly expensive, the yield is high, so the resulting crop of sprouts is quite reasonable in price.

ALMOND. Unhulled almonds are not easy to find but, if you do locate some in a health or Oriental food store, they are delicious sprouted and used as you would any nut meat. Soak for twice as long as other seeds —about 24 hours, rinse often and keep quite wet. A sprouting time of 3 to 5 days will give you 1/8 to 1/4 inch sprouts, which are just right for use.

BARLEY. This is one of the oldest of all known grains, its origin is lost in man's own prehistoric beginnings. Barley formed a part of the religious rites for many Old World peoples. Once a mainstay in bread making, its use today is largely confined to the brewing of alcoholic beverages and to livestock feed. However, barley sprouts have a fine nut-like flavor that makes them suitable for use anywhere you would use wheat, oats or rice—particularly in breads, soups and casserole dishes. Treat as you would wheat, oats or millet sprouts. Sprouting time is 3 to 5 days; use when sprouted length is no longer than the seed.

BEANS—Black, Broad, Fava, Kidney, Lima, Navy, Pea, Pinto and Red (see also *MUNG BEANS* and *SOYBEANS*). The bean kingdom is one of the most varied in the plant world and beans range in size from limas and kidneys, which are nearly an inch long, to pea beans, no more than 3/8 inch long. Almost every country has some traditional dish made with beans and, by the same token, all have their body of folklore about beans, even to the extent of thinking of them as unlucky. Under most conditions the bean is a prolific producer and the peoples of

South America and the Orient still rely on beans as a staple item of diet. Sprouted beans lose the gas-producing quality of the unsprouted bean and become readily digestible. Each variety of bean sprout has a distinctive taste and all are most adaptable to every kind of use—in appetizers, breads, drinks, main dishes, salads and soup. Most of the bean sprouts listed here are as good raw as they are cooked. Sprouting time for most beans is 3 to 5 days and sprouted length should be ½ to 1½ inches, depending on the bean. A good rule of thumb for beans is "the larger the bean, the shorter the sprout." Larger bean sprouts tend to be tougher and smaller ones more tender, so try different lengths for each bean and select the length and flavor you prefer.

BROCCOLI see *CABBAGE FAMILY*

BRUSSELS SPROUTS see *CABBAGE FAMILY*

BUCKWHEAT. Buckwheat is one of the fastest growing of all grain or cereal crops. For centuries it was used throughout Russia, Manchuria and Europe in bread making. It is less extensively grown in the United States than in the past, which is unfortunate because it is almost totally free of disease or blight. Most of the American crop is used in pancake flours and livestock feed, while buckwheat honey is relished for its distinctive taste and dark color. Buckwheat kernels tend to stick together, so rinse rather than soak them and sprinkle often to keep moist. Sprouting time is rather short—2 to 4 days usually. Some people prefer their buckwheat sprouts no longer than the grain itself—¼ to ½ inch—and others like a sprout ¾ to 1 inch long. Buckwheat sprouts can be used in any recipe that calls for barley, millet, oat, rice or wheat sprouts, e.g., breads, cereals, main dishes and soups.

CABBAGE FAMILY—Broccoli, Brussels sprouts, Cabbage, Cauliflower, Collards and Kale. The cabbage family has almost as many relatives as the bean family. All are easy to sprout and each one produces a tasty sprout of a slightly different flavor. Not everyone likes every kind of sprout from the cabbage family, so experiment with a few seeds at a time. Sprouting time is 3 to 5 days for a sprouted length of ½ to 1 inch. One word of caution, these sprouts tend to become strong flavored or bitter if grown too long, so use them when they are most pleasant to

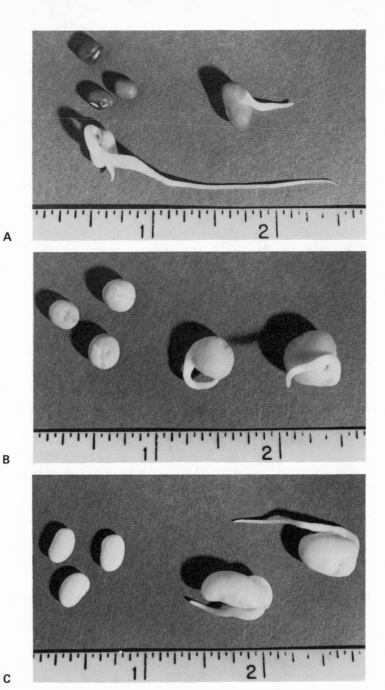

The photos above and on the following pages give a good idea of the relative size and appearance of many of the most favored
10   seeds to sprout and their resultant sprouts.

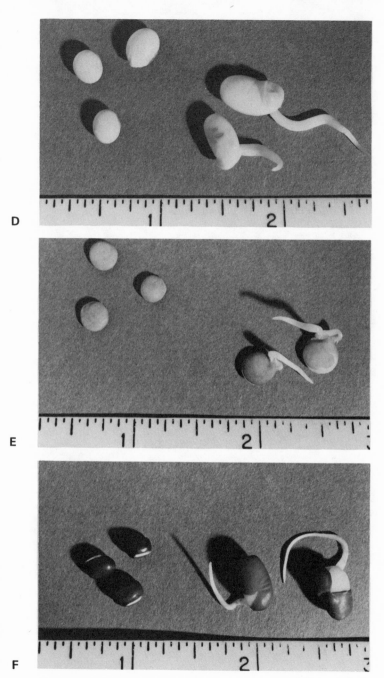

The seeds and sprouts shown here are: A, Mung Bean; B, Pea; C, Pea Bean; D, Soybean; E, Lentil and F, Adzuki. Scaled to the ruler, most are pictured at the size recommended for best use.   11

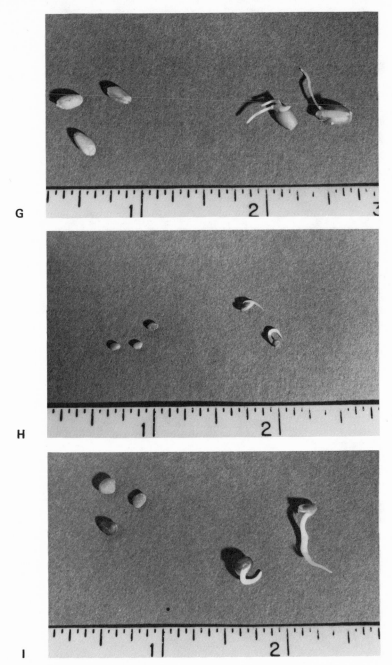

More seeds and sprouts. Shown on this spread are: G, Wheat;
12   H, Alfalfa; I, Radish; J, Rye; K, Cauliflower and L, Corn.

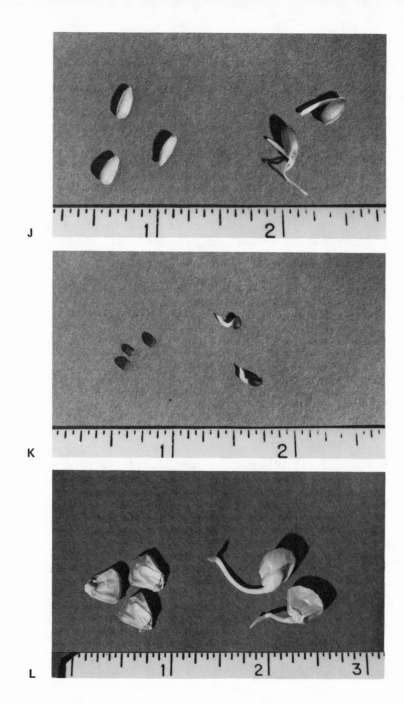

your taste in soups, salads and main dishes. Like their parent plants, they are high in vitamins and so are well worth sprouting.

CAULIFLOWER see *CABBAGE FAMILY*

CHIA. Chia seeds come from one of the family of sage plants and are not well known outside of Mexico and the American Southwest. Nor are they easy to sprout, being somewhat gluey so that they stick together when moist. However, aficionados rave about the slightly pungent taste they add to salads and sandwich spreads and point to their high trace-mineral content. So, if you are able to locate chia seeds and decide to try them, do so in moderation. But don't try to soak them; they will stick together in an unmanageable mass. Put the seeds on a saucer or small plate, sprinkle with water and let stand overnight. Another way is to put a small amount of water on a plate and float the seeds on top. Sprinkle again as the seeds dry out. Sprouting time is usually 1 or 2 days for 1/8-to 1/4-inch sprouts, which is the best length for most uses.

CHICKPEA. The chickpea, as it is called in the United States, is known by many names elsewhere in the world, garbanzo being one of the most common. The plant is highly drought resistant, which makes it ideal for growing in the subtropics, as well as the drier sections of Europe and North America. Nearly, although not quite, as high in protein as soybean sprouts, chickpea sprouts can be used in any dish that calls for the former. Chickpeas should also be sprouted the same way as soybeans —rinsing about 4 to 6 times in 24 hours because they tend to spoil quickly if left wet for any length of time without rinsing. Sprouting time is generally about 5 to 8 days and sprouted length about ¾ to 1 inch.

CLOVER. The red clover seed is the one you want for sprouting. Handle it the same way as alfalfa and use it in the same kind of recipes; i.e., when the sprouts are just the length of the seed, they are best for appetizers, cereals and breads but when grown to 1-inch length and greened in sunlight use them in salads.

CORN. Untreated corn seed is almost never available, so two possibilities are open to the sprouter. Buy the whole field corn used for animal feed or raise your own sweet corn and let some of it mature for drying and later sprouting. The latter course will give you the best product. For sprouting, many people prefer the variety of corn known as Deaf Smith County but any sweet corn that you enjoy fresh will be palatable as sprouted corn. Try adding corn sprouts to soups or casseroles. Steam some and serve buttered as a side-dish vegetable. Oven-dried and finely ground corn sprouts may be used to replace part or all of the cornmeal in a quick-bread recipe. The possibilities are limited only by the inventiveness of the cook. Sprouting time can vary from 3 to 8 days, depending on the variety of seed used. Sprouted length should be ½ to 1 inch.

CRESS. A fast-growing plant with a peppery taste, its leaves are most often used in sandwiches or salads. Cress sprouts may be used in the same way but with moderation because of their pungency. Somewhat gluey like chia seeds, cress seeds should be sprouted the same way and harvested when the sprout is about ¾ to 1 inch long, usually after 2 to 4 days.

FENUGREEK. This member of the legume family is almost unknown in the Western hemisphere but in the Far East it is used for seasoning, particularly in curry powder. The seeds sprout readily and in 3 or 4 days will reach ½-inch length, which is just about right to bring out Fenugreek's spicy flavor. Any longer in the sprouting process and the sprouts get bitter tasting.

FLAX. Flax is one of man's most helpful folk remedies for use in poultices and cough syrups, while the fiber is used to make linen. Flax seed is slightly gluey and should be sprouted like chia. Grown to ¾- or 1-inch length—a length which usually takes 3 or 4 days of growing time—flax sprouts make a mild-flavored and delicate addition to salads and soups. If desired, they may be grown somewhat longer and greened in the sunlight for 3 or 4 hours to be used as you would any salad greens.

GARBANZO see *CHICKPEA*

LENTIL. One of the oldest vegetables known to man, lentils are mentioned in the Bible as the food for which Esau sold his birthright to Jacob. There are many different strains of lentil, ranging in color from green to yellow and redish brown. They sprout easily and even those bought in grocery stores will usually make good sprouts if the cracked and broken seeds are discarded. They taste best when grown to the length of the seed—about ¼ or ½ inch—which generally takes about 3 or 4 days. Use lentil sprouts in soups, stews, main dishes and,steamed very briefly, as a side-dish vegetable.

MELON see *PUMPKIN*

MILLET. Another one of the cereal grains, millet, can be sprouted like barley. Use the millet sprouts in the same way as barley, oat, or wheat sprouts—in soups, cereals, breads, vegetable side-dishes and main-dish meals. Sprouting time is 3 to 5 days and the sprout should be used when it is about seed length.

MUNG BEAN. This is the seed to start with if sprouting is a new thing for you. It is almost impossible to go wrong in growing mung bean sprouts as long as they are not allowed to dry out. The Chinese have sprouted the tiny mung bean for 3,000 years and it forms the basis for much Oriental cooking. A sprouting time of 3 or 4 days will give shoots about 1 inch long, but the sprouts may be eaten any time from the point when they emerge from the seed up to about 3 inches in length. They are delicious raw in salads; steamed for 1 or 2 minutes they are a superb side-dish vegetable—low in calories and high in nutrition. In combination with many other foods they are used in many dishes, as you will see in the recipe section of this book.

OAT. Only unhulled oats are used for sprouting and with very little water in the sprouting process. It is best not to presoak oats, but to rinse them quickly and then dampen only once a day until the sprout is the length of the seed, usually in 3 to 5 days. Oat sprouts are used in the same way as barley, millet, rice and wheat sprouts in breads, cereals and main-dish meals.

PEA. Peas come in almost as many varieties as beans. Any kind of whole pea seeds can be sprouted, following the basic directions for bean and lentil seeds. The smaller the sprout, the more tender it will be, so peas should be sprouted for 3 or 4 days and eaten when the sprout is about the length of the seed. Pea sprouts may be used in the same ways as traditional fresh or dried peas.

PUMPKIN. Oriental people have long eaten the seeds of pumpkins, squash and the larger melons. They are loaded with food value. So, if you can find any of these seeds in raw, unhulled form at an Oriental food store, or elsewhere, try sprouting a few until the sprout has just barely emerged—3 to 5 days. Toast them lightly in a moderate oven and eat them as a snack, or chop and add to desserts, candy or breads.

RADISH. Radish seeds, like mustard seeds, tend to be rather expensive for sprouting but you only need a few sprouts at a time to use in conjunction with other less peppery vegetables or greens. And they do add a pleasant and tangy radishy taste to salads, soups and vegetable dishes. As one way around the expense, and since radishes mature so quickly, home gardeners may want to let a few plants mature fully and then harvest the seeds for later sprouting. Radish sprouts are best at ½ to 1 inch long which usually takes 2 to 4 days growing time.

RICE. Rice forms the main part of the diet for half the world's people but only whole-grain brown rice can be sprouted; white or polished rice has had the seed's protective coating removed. The bland flavor of rice lends itself well to use with other foods. Rice sprouts are no exception to this rule. They are both delicious and extremely versatile and may be used in the same ways as barley, millet, oats, rye and wheat sprouts in breads, cereals, soups and main dishes. The sprouts are best at seed length which usually takes about 3 or 4 days.

RYE. Rye is very similar to wheat and barley in its sprouting qualities and taste. Rye sprouts are ready to eat when the sprout is the length of the seed in about 3 to 5 days sprouting time. Use seed-length rye sprouts in cereals, breads, soups and main dishes. If you are going to use rye sprouts for salads, let them grow to 1 or 1½ inches and green in sunlight for a few hours to allow the chlorophyll to develop.

SESAME. Most people are familiar with sesame seeds in breads and pastries. Unhulled sesame seeds, sprouted until the bud is just barely visible—about 3 days sprouting time—are delicious; but sesame sprouts become very bitter if allowed to develop longer. Toasted lightly, sesame sprouts are delightful in breads and desserts. Use just as you would the un-sprouted seeds.

SOYBEAN. Although soybeans have been a major source of protein in the Orient for hundreds of years, only in the past 40 to 50 years have they become well known in the United States. The list of products —both food and industrial—that are created from soybeans staggers the imagination. The literature about soybeans is enormous and several good, popular works have been written on the nutrition they offer. For the purposes of this book, let it suffice to say that soybean sprouts are one of the best of all meat substitutes. They contain up to 40 percent protein, large amounts of Vitamin C and many other nutrients essential for human health. However, soybeans are somewhat difficult to sprout. It is a good idea to gain a little familiarity with sprouting mung beans, peas and one of the grains, say wheat or rye, before trying soybeans. The seeds must be kept moist to sprout but the moisture can cause them to ferment quickly—especially in hot summer weather—so they must be rinsed frequently in large amounts of water preferably 4 to 6 times in every 24 hours. It is also important to pick out any beans that do not show signs of sprouting properly because they can cause the whole batch to spoil. Soybean sprouts generally develop to about 1 inch—the favored length for eating either raw or cooked—in 4 to 6 days. Some people enjoy the taste of raw soybean sprouts, but most find the taste a little strong so you will probably want to cook them according to the various suggestions in the recipe section of this book.

SQUASH see *PUMPKIN*

SUNFLOWER. The Incas held the sunflower in mystical reverence because of the plant's unusual trait of keeping its face always to the sun and then bowing its head when the sun sets. Sunflower seeds are a rich source of unsaturated oils and trace elements. Unhulled seeds are the kind to get for sprouting and, like sesame seeds, sunflower seeds must be sprouted only until the bud is just barely visible, otherwise the sprout becomes very strong and bitter tasting. This usually takes from 5 to 8 days. However, some varieties take longer than others to sprout, so be patient and keep them somewhat warmer than you do other seeds—75 to 80 degrees is just about right.

TRITICALE. This is the newest development in grains, being a cross between wheat and rye and higher in protein than either parent grain.

It should be sprouted and used as one would wheat or rye, except that it sprouts in less time, usually reaching the preferred seed length in 1 to 3 days.

WHEAT. Wheat forms a larger part of the diet for more people on earth than any other grain. In the whole grain form, wheat is also one of the most nourishing of all plant foods. Whole-grain wheat is what you want for sprouting. It is one of the cheapest of all seeds to buy; it is easy to sprout and has a very high yield. One cup of wheat will produce a full quart of wheat sprouts the length of the seeds themselves in 4 to 5 days. Highly versatile, wheat sprouts lend themselves to use in cereals, breads, appetizers, soups, salads, vegetable dishes and main dishes, as well as in a few desserts.

Warning—only chemically untreated and certified edible seeds should be used for sprouting.

Sprouting Your Seeds

A seed is a wonderful packet from Nature containing a live—but dormant—embryo plant and enough food reserves to nourish the embryo until it develops the ability to manufacture its own food from the moisture, light and soil nutrients it finds around it as it grows.

Each seed is encased in a tough outer shell or husk. When the right combination of warmth, moisture and light is provided (generally speaking, an absense of light is best), the seed swells, bursts its shell and starts to grow. That is what sprouting is all about: establishing the right amount of moisture and the correct temperature and light conditions to enable the seed to sprout.

Seeds need relative darkness to sprout best, so if your sprouting containers are transparent you should put them in a dark place. The cupboard under most sinks is a good place. Barring that, try the oven —but only if it's electric and the heat is not on (the pilot light rules out a gas stove).

Because certain gases are released by the sprouting process, a free flow of air should be provided for the growing seeds. This can best be achieved by not overcrowding: a few layers of seeds in a large container is much better than several layers in a small one. And frequent rinsing also helps to keep the seeds sweet and sprouting at their best.

Equipment

Everyone who has had any experience with sprouting has a favorite method or methods, often depending upon the seed to be sprouted. There is a large variety of equipment on the market for use in sprouting. One such item is an ingenious plastic container made in Switzerland

A sampling of sprouting containers. Starting at nine o'clock, clockwise, they are: A many-tiered plastic sprouter; a canning jar with a wire-mesh lid; a covered earthenware container and a second jar, topped with cheesecloth.

known as the Bio-Snacky Sprouter. It consists of 5 parts—the container itself, 3 suspended sprouting trays, and a top. Less elaborate but also effective is a shallow, covered unglazed earthenware container. Other ready-made sprouting equipment available include special jar tops fitted with wire mesh that screw onto regulation-size jars.

Actually no special equipment is required for sprouting. A great many household utensils make excellent sprouting containers: shallow bowls that can be covered; wide-mouth jars that can be fitted with a square of cheesecloth or mesh (a nylon stocking works particularly well) and held in place with rubber bands; plastic refrigerator or storage containers, preferably with covers; clean flower pots, the wider and shallower the better, with the center drainage hole plugged; aluminum foil pans such as those that frozen prepared foods come in, with holes punched in the bottom for drainage. Just plain dampened white paper toweling is often preferred for sprouting smaller seeds.

The Method

The general technique for sprouting most seeds is as follows:

1. Carefully pick over the seeds you are going to sprout, discarding any that are cracked, broken or discolored. One-quarter cupful is a good amount to start with; this many seeds from the cereal, grain, cabbage, pea or bean families will produce about 1 to 2 cups of finished sprouts —enough for 4 average servings.

2. Rinse the seeds thoroughly. A strainer or sieve is handy at this point.

3. Put the washed seeds in a bowl, jar or other container that does not have a hole in the bottom.

4. Cover the seeds with cool to lukewarm water at least 4 times the depth of the seeds. In this initial soaking process, the seeds will rapidly absorb moisture and increase greatly in volume. Leave the seeds in water overnight.

5. In the morning, pour off the soaking water. Some people throw it out, while others recommend using it as a base for soups. (One sprouter tried using the soak-water on her house plants and reported greatly increased growth.)

6. Put the drained seeds in the sprouting container—a shallow bowl with paper towels in the bottom; a mesh-covered jar tilted at an angle to allow it to drain; an aluminum foil pan with drain holes punched in the bottom; a flower pot with the center drainage hole plugged, or whatever you have decided to use. The important point is to allow the seeds to stay slightly damp, without standing in water and, at the same time, to let them "breathe." (The very smallest seeds will do very well between double layers of dampened white paper towels, but be sure to rinse them in a fine strainer from time to time.)

7. Morning and night the seeds should be rinsed in clear water, and then inspected. Any seeds that are not sprouting properly should be discarded. The rest should be drained and returned to their sprouting container. Chickpeas and soybeans must be rinsed 4 to 6 times within each 24-hour period because they tend to spoil very quickly particularly in hot summer weather.

No matter which container is used, sprouting seeds must be kept moist. Here, water is poured into a pie plate placed under an earthenware sprouter. Moisture is then absorbed by the seeds through the porous clay.

Small seeds often do better with a different sprouting technique. One way is to shake the soaked seeds directly onto a moist paper towel, then cover lightly with another towel and sprinkle to keep moist.

Proper rinsing is an essential step in successful sprouting. Top left, rinsing in the tray of a plastic sprouter, the water will seep out through a small hole in the bottom; at right, making sure the sprouts are evenly distributed after rinsing; bottom left, using a cheesecloth-covered jar; at right, through a wire-mesh lid.

Rinsing small seeds can pose a problem; they can stick to their containers. At left, the old water is poured off fledgling alfalfa sprouts; at right, fresh rinse water is run through the sprouts in a small strainer.

During the sprouting process, the outer case or husk of the seed will gradually loosen. Generally speaking, you will want to float the husks away in the rinsing process. But do it gently; many seeds tend to split into their two halves if the husk is wrenched away and the seed will then not continue to sprout properly. If the sprouts are to be cooked, you may find you do not object to the husks on some of the more tender varieties. So try your sprouts with and without the husks and decide for yourself.

8. Most seeds will sprout properly at temperatures ranging from 60 to 80 degrees; in short, at normal household temperatures. Soybeans and chickpeas are the exceptions; they will do as well, if not better, at somewhat lower temperatures, so try to keep them cool while they sprout.

Seeds sprout better in the dark;
a cupboard is a good place.

Many sprouts—especially soybeans—
are better with their husks removed,
particularly when to be used raw.

9. Although the sprouting process should take place in a dark situation, the cereals and grains—alfalfa, rye, clover, wheat, rye, barley and millet—may be allowed a few hours in either artificial light or indirect sunlight after their initial sprouting to let them develop chlorophyll. This is called "greening" and a good many people enjoy the slightly sweet fresh-green taste of the resulting "grass." A sprout length of 1 to 2 inches is generally good for this stage of growth.

10. A good sprouting plan is to start a different kind of seed every day or two. As the sprouts reach the desired length, rinse them once more, drain well and refrigerate in tightly closed plastic containers or bags. Sprouts will keep well under refrigeration for 4 to 6 days, just as any other fresh vegetable.

11. If you have more sprouts on hand at any time than you can use while they are still fresh, oven-dry (actually, roast) them for future use in any of the many recipes in this book that call for oven-dried sprouts. Soybean, cereal, grain, rice and corn sprouts dry particularly well. The procedure is as follows: drain the sprouts thoroughly; put them on thick layers of paper towels and gently blot to remove as much moisture as possible; spread the sprouts loosely, and only one layer deep, on cookie sheets; place them in a 325 to 350 oven, leaving the door slightly open; stir the sprouts from time to time so that the hot air reaches all evenly.

Depending on the kind of sprout and the amount of moisture in the air, the sprouts will generally be dry enough in 1 to 3 hours. When dry, either grind coarsely in a food grinder or leave whole. Store in closed containers in a dry, dark, cool place (they may be refrigerated in hot weather) and use as needed to give a sweet nut-like flavor to many different foods.

A good way to use a surplus supply of sprouts is to oven-roast and grind them to save for later use. Here we see already toasted soybean sprouts about to be ground and a sample of the finished product.

Some recipes call for sprouts to be ground before using. Here soybean sprouts are being put through a food mill.

Once the sprouting is finished, the cooking can begin. This shot shows mung bean sprouts being stir-fried, a frequent step in sprout cookery.

Warning—only chemically untreated
and certified edible seeds should be
used for sprouting.

A Final Word

Make sprouting a family project. Many children are fascinated by the sprouting process, so let them sprout a few seeds of their own. It may make sprout eaters out of the most confirmed anti-vegetable youngsters. This may work best if you let them try a few of the sprouts that are particularly good raw—one of the grains, for example, that can be oven-dried and toasted for a healthful between-meal snack.

And, as a final word of encouragement, don't think that a great amount of time needs to be spent on sprouting. A minute or two morning and night for rinsing and draining the sprouting seeds is all that is required to provide you and your family with an abundance of garden-fresh food all year long.

QUICK-REFERENCE SPROUTING TABLE

SEED	DESIRED SPROUT LENGTH	AVERAGE SPROUTING TIME	SPROUT YIELD (in lengths given in column 1)		PROPER SPROUTING METHOD	EAT RAW?	AVERAGE COOKING TIME
			seeds used	sprouts obtained			
ADZUKI	½–1 in.	4–5 days	¼ c.	1 c.	soak & rinse	yes	8–12 min.
ALFALFA	seed length	1–2 days*	1 c.	2½ c.	soak & rinse	yes	3–5 min.
ALMOND	1/8–1/4 in.	3–5 days	¼ c.	½ c.	soak & rinse		oven roast
BARLEY	seed length	3–5 days	½ c.	1 c.	soak & rinse		8–10 min.
BEANS₁	½–1½ in.	3–5 days	¼ c.	1¼ c.	soak & rinse	yes	8–15 min.
BUCKWHEAT	seed length	2–4 days	1 c.	2½ c.	rinse & sprinkle only		8–15 min.
CABBAGE₂	½–1 in.	3–5 days	¼ c.	1¼ c.	soak & rinse	yes	3–8 min.
CHIA	1/8–1/4 in.	1–2 days	¼ c.	1 c.	sprinkle only	yes	
CHICKPEA₃	¾–1 in.	5–8 days	1 c.	3½ c.	soak & rinse†	yes	10–20 min.
CLOVER	seed length	1–2 days*	1 c.	2½ c.	soak & rinse	yes	3–5 min.
CORN	½–1 in.	3–8 days	¼ c.	1¼ c.	soak & rinse		5–12 min.
CRESS	¾–1 in.	2–4 days	1 T.	¾ c.	sprinkle only	yes	
FENUGREEK	½ in.	3–4 days	¼ c.	1 c.	soak & rinse	yes	2–4 min.
FLAX	¾–1 in.	3–4 days	1 T.	¾ c.	sprinkle only	yes	2–4 min.
LENTIL	¼–½ in.	3–4 days	1 c.	2 c.	soak & rinse		3–8 min.
MILLET	seed length	3–5 days	1 c.	2½ c.	soak & rinse		8–10 min.
MUNG BEAN	½–3 in.	3–8 days	1 c.	4 c.	soak & rinse	yes	2–5 min.

OAT	seed length	3–5 days	1 c.	2½ c.	sprinkle only		8–10 min.
PEA	¼–½ in.	3–4 days	1 c.	2 c.	soak & rinse		3–8 min.
PUMPKIN₄	budded only	3–5 days	1 c.	1½ c.	soak & rinse		oven roast
RADISH	½–1 in.	2–4 days	1 T.	¾ c.	soak & rinse	yes	8–10 min.
RICE	seed length	3–4 days	1 c.	2½ c.	soak & rinse		8–10 min.
RYE	seed length	3–5 days*	1 c.	2½ c.	soak & rinse	yes	3–5 min.
SESAME	budded only	2–3 days	¼ c.	½ c.	soak & rinse		oven roast
SOYBEAN	¾–1 in.	4–6 days	1 c.	3½ c.	soak & rinse†	yes	10–20 min.
SUNFLOWER	budded only	5–8 days	1 c.	2 c.	soak & rinse		oven roast
TRITICALE	seed length	1–3 days	1 c.	3 c.	soak & rinse	yes	8–10 min.
WHEAT	seed length	4–5 days	1 c.	4 c.	soak & rinse	yes	8–10 min.

* ALFALFA, CLOVER and RYE sprouts may be allowed to grow to 1 or 2 inches, then greened in sunlight for 3 or 4 hours and used as salad greens, if desired.

† CHICKPEA and SOYBEAN need to be rinsed 4 to 6 times within every 24 hours because they tend to ferment or spoil quickly.

1 BEANS include BLACK, BROAD, FAVA, KIDNEY, LIMA, NAVY, PEA, PINTO and RED varieties.

2 CABBAGE includes other members of the same family—BROCCOLI, BRUSSELS SPROUTS, CABBAGE, CAULIFLOWER, COLLARDS and KALE.

3 CHICKPEAS are also known as GARBANZOS.

4 PUMPKIN, MELON and SQUASH are treated the same way.

Recipes

appetizers

Sprout Fritters

(10 to 20 Fritters)

Served hot and skewered on toothpicks, these are yummy for snacks or as hot hors d'oeuvres. They also can be served as a vegetarian main dish for dinner or lunch.

1 cup Wheat or Rice Sprouts
1 small onion
1/3 cup peanuts, walnuts or almonds
1 cup bread crumbs (whole wheat are best)
½ cup milk or vegetable stock
½ teaspoon salt
pinch of pepper
oil for frying

Grind rather finely the sprouts, onion and nuts. Add bread crumbs (made from *Sprouted Whole Wheat Bread* or *Sprout and Bran Muffins,* if possible), milk or vegetable stock, salt and pepper. Mix thoroughly and shape into 1-inch balls. Heat oil for deep-fat frying. Fry a few fritters at a time very quickly—about 1 or 2 minutes—until crisp and brown. Drain on paper and serve hot. If necessary, the fritters can be fried for a somewhat shorter time, cooled, refrigerated or frozen, and heated in the oven just before serving.

Sprout Stuffed Eggs

(2 or 3 Servings)

½ cup Mung Bean Sprouts
3 or 4 hard-boiled eggs
1 teaspoon soy sauce
1 teaspoon salad oil or mayonnaise
¼ teaspoon curry powder
2 or 3 drops Tabasco or Worcestershire sauce
salt and pepper to taste
paprika or chopped parsley

Cut eggs in half lengthwise and put yolks in small bowl. Chop sprouts fine and combine with egg yolks. Mix well. Add soy sauce, salad oil or mayonnaise, curry powder, Tabasco or Worcestershire sauce, and salt and pepper. Stuff egg whites with mixture. Garnish with paprika or parsley and chill well before serving.

Sprout Stuffed Tomatoes

(2 to 4 Servings)

You can use any sprout available for this recipe. The results are delicious, so make lots.

½ cup sprouts (Mung Bean, Pea, Lentil, Alfalfa,
   Wheat, Fenugreek)
10 or 12 cocktail or cherry tomatoes
1 tablespoon salad oil or mayonnaise
3 or 4 drops lemon juice
1 tablespoon minced chives, or other herbs
¼ teaspoon salt

Take small slice off top of each tomato and scoop out inside with melon baller. Chop sprouts very fine and add tomato pulp. Add remaining ingredients and mix thoroughly. Stuff tomato shells with mixture. Chill thoroughly before serving.

Variation: sprinkle stuffed tomatoes with liberal amount of grated cheese and quick-broil on crisp toast squares for tasty hot hors d'oeuvres.

Stuffed Mushrooms

(2 to 4 Servings)

½ cup Wheat, Bean or Alfalfa Sprouts
8 or 10 large fresh mushrooms
1 tablespoon finely minced onion
1 raw egg yolk
¼ cup grated cheese
1 tablespoon wheat germ
salt, pepper and celery salt to taste

Wash and stem the mushrooms, reserving stems for use in another sprout dish. Chop the sprouts very fine and add remaining ingredients. Mix well and stuff hollow side of mushrooms with sprout mixture. Broil for about 8 minutes and serve piping hot.

Cream Cheese-Sprout Puffs

(2 to 4 Servings)

Children like these just as well as adults do.

¼ cup sprouts (Alfalfa, Cabbage, Bean, Pea,
  Mustard, Radish)
4 frozen patty shells
4 ounces cream cheese
1 egg, well beaten
1 or 2 drops Tabasco or Worcestershire sauce
1 tablespoon chopped chives
few drops salad oil

Bake patty shells according to directions. Let cream cheese soften at room temperature. Add beaten egg, finely chopped sprouts, Tabasco or Worcestershire sauce, chives and a few drops of salad oil. Whip with fork until mixture is light and creamy. Fill shells and bake at 400 until cheese is puffed up and golden brown on top—about 20 to 25 minutes. Serve immediately.

Sweet and Sour Sprouts

(2 or 3 Servings)

Weight watchers will appreciate this low calorie dish for an appetizer or as an accompaniment to a rather bland meal.

    1½ cups Mung Bean Sprouts
    1/3 cup vinegar (either cider or wine)
    1/3 cup water
    1 tablespoon vegetable oil
    1 small onion, sliced very thin
    1 tablespoon sugar (or equivalent sugar substitute)
    ½ teaspoon salt
    pinch of pepper

Combine all ingredients in bowl or glass jar. Cover and refrigerate for at least 4 hours (mixture may be kept in refrigerator for a week). Drain and serve plain.

Variation idea: try different kinds of sprouts—Alfalfa, Cabbage family, Pea and Bean families (note: Soybean sprouts are somewhat tough, so they should be precooked for 10 to 12 minutes).

Soy Snacks No. 1

(2 Cups)

Let both children and adults try these as a substitute for nuts.

    2 cups Soybean Sprouts
    oil for frying
    salt

Soak sprouts in ice cold water for a few minutes. Drain and towel dry. Deep-fry a few sprouts at a time in hot fat until golden brown (fat will bubble, so go easy). Drain well and sprinkle with salt—sea salt tastes best. Cool and serve as you would salted nuts.

Variation: try seasoned salt instead of table or sea salt.

Avocado-Cucumber Slices

(2 to 4 Servings)

This is another recipe for which any available sprout is fine.

> 2/3 cup sprouts (Alfalfa, Pea, Bean, Wheat,
>   Cabbage, Radish)
> 1 medium-size cucumber
> 1 small avocado
> 1 or 2 cherry tomatoes
> 1 tablespoon lemon juice
> 1 teaspoon minced chives
> salt and pepper to taste
> small amount of wheat germ

Remove small slice from each end of cucumber and lightly score the skin lengthwise. With melon baller or small scoop remove seeds and some of the cucumber pulp. Discard. In a small bowl mash the avocado and beat with a fork until creamy. Add finely chopped sprouts and chopped tomatoes, lemon juice, chives, salt and pepper. If the mixture is too wet, add a little wheat germ. Mix thoroughly and pack into hollow cucumber. Refrigerate for several hours and then slice crosswise with a very sharp knife. Arrange for serving alternately with *Rye Sprout Crisps.*

Soy Snacks No. 2

(2 Cups)

If you are trying to eliminate fats, this is a good method.

> 2 cups Soybean Sprouts
> salt

Soak sprouts in ice cold water for a few minutes. Drain and towel dry. Arrange sprouts in a single layer on baking sheet. Bake in 350 oven for about 25 or 30 minutes—until golden brown. Salt and let cool before serving.

Sole and Sprout Appetizer

(2 to 4 Servings)

½ cup Mung Bean Sprouts
½ cup sole, poached and flaked
2 or 3 thin slices Bermuda onion
1 stalk celery, sliced very thin
2 tablespoons sour cream or yogurt
1 tablespoon lemon juice
pinch of pepper
pinch of garlic powder
salt to taste
1 large tomato
chopped parsley for garnish

Mix sprouts, sole, onion, celery, sour cream or yogurt, lemon juice and seasonings in a bowl. Refrigerate for several hours to marinate flavors. When ready to serve, heap sprout and sole mixture on thick slices of chilled tomato and garnish with chopped parsley.

Variation idea: for a different taste, add 2 or 3 tablespoons finely chopped cucumber and/or a pinch of oregano to the mixture, omitting the garlic powder.

Cheese and Sprout Dip

(About 1½ Cups)

1 cup Alfalfa or Fenugreek Sprouts, chopped
4 ounces cream cheese
2 or 3 tablespoons yogurt or light cream
¼ cup finely chopped chives
½ teaspoon celery seed
½ teaspoon salt

Soften cream cheese at room temperature. Add remaining ingredients. Whip well with fork until light and fluffy, adding more yogurt or light cream if necessary.

Yogurt and Sprout Dip

(About 1½ Cups)

Any available sprouts can be used for this tangy dip.

2/3 cup sprouts
1 cup plain yogurt
¼ cup finely minced onion or scallion
½ teaspoon salt
pepper to taste

Mix all ingredients together. Chill thoroughly and serve.

Avocado and Sprout Dip

(About 1½ Cups)

1 cup Mung Bean Sprouts
1 avocado
1 egg yolk, well beaten
1 tablespoon salad oil or mayonnaise
1 strip bacon, fried crisp and crumbled
salt and pepper to taste

Mash avocado in bowl. Add egg and salad oil or mayonnaise. Whip with fork. Add sprouts, bacon crumbles, salt and pepper. Serve chilled.

Cheese Sprout Balls

(2 to 4 Servings)

½ cup Wheat Sprouts
4 ounces cream cheese
½ teaspoon salt
¼ teaspoon onion powder
1/3 cup chopped nuts or toasted sesame seeds

Soften cream cheese at room temperature. Add sprouts, salt and onion powder. Shape into 1-inch balls. Roll in chopped nuts or seeds. Chill thoroughly before serving.

Cucumber and Sprout Dip

(About 1½ Cups)

½ cup Radish or Fenugreek Sprouts
4 ounces cream cheese
1 small cucumber
1 tablespoon chopped chives or scallion
1 teaspoon salt
milk or light cream as needed

Soften cream cheese at room temperature in a small bowl. Cut cucumber in half lengthwise, remove and discard seeds and center fibers. Shred or grate the remainder of the cucumber. Add sprouts, cucumber, chives or scallion and salt to the cream cheese. Add a few drops of milk or light cream as needed and whip until fluffy. Chill before serving.

This same mixture, prepared with less liquid, makes an excellent sandwich spread—especially if used on a sprout bread.

Mushroom and Sprout Dip

(About 1½ Cups)

1½ cups Mung Bean Sprouts, chopped
2 tablespoons butter or margarine
¾ cup mushroom stems and pieces (fresh or canned)
2 tablespoons chopped chives
2 tablespoons chopped parsley
2 or 3 tablespoons water
salt to taste

Sauté mushrooms in fat until golden brown. Chop finely and add to sprouts. Add remaining ingredients, using as much water (or juice from mushrooms, if canned were used) as needed to make dipping consistency.

For a delightfully different taste treat and a change from the conventional cracker—try serving this dip with celery stalks and carrot sticks.

Blended Sprout Spread

(About 1½ Cups)

This is a good basic spread that can be made ahead and kept in the refrigerator for up to a week. With the addition of shredded seafood, chopped eggs, olives, pickles or meat, it can form the basis for quick hors d'oeuvres. Add a little cream cheese or more oil and it can be used as a dip.

> 1 cup Alfalfa, Cabbage, Clover or Radish Sprouts
> ½ cup Mung Bean Sprouts
> ½ cup Navy, Pinto, Kidney, or Garbanzo Bean Sprouts
> 1 small onion
> 2 to 4 tablespoons vegetable oil
> 1 to 2 tablespoons lemon juice
> salt to taste

Grind sprouts and onion medium to fine. Blend in oil, lemon juice and salt. Keep in refrigerator until ready to serve.

Soy Sprout Butter

(About 3/4 Cup)

This is a fine substitute for peanut butter and can be used in exactly the same way.

> 1 cup Soybean Sprouts, well toasted
> peanut, safflower or corn oil, as needed
> salt to taste

Grind the toasted sprouts very fine. Add oil drop by drop until mixture is the consistency you want. Salt to taste. If chunky butter is desired, add a few coarsely ground toasted sprouts after blending is done.

soups

Meatball and Sprout Soup

(2 to 4 Servings)

1 cup Wheat or Rye Sprouts
¼ cup bread crumbs
¼ cup milk
2 tablespoons chopped onion
¼ pound liverwurst
3 cups chicken or beef broth
salt and pepper to taste

Moisten bread crumbs with milk. Add chopped onion and liverwurst and mix well. Form into small meatballs and drop into rapidly boiling chicken or beef broth. Add sprouts and cook for 15 to 20 minutes. Season to taste and serve with toasted onion or garlic bread.

Beef and Lentil Soup

(2 to 4 Servings)

1½ cups Lentil Sprouts
1 tablespoon cooking oil or butter
1 small onion, chopped
½ cup raw beef, or leftover meat, cubed
3 cups beef broth or bouillon
¼ cup shredded carrot
¼ cup chopped celery
1 teaspoon salt
pepper to taste

Sauté beef and onion in cooking oil or butter. Add beef broth or bouillon. Bring to boiling point. Add Lentil sprouts, shredded carrot, chopped celery, salt and pepper. Simmer covered for 20 to 30 minutes.

Beef and Bean Sprout Soup

(2 to 4 Servings)

A nice, light, clear soup that serves equally well as a luncheon dish or as the soup course for dinner.

2 cups Mung Bean Sprouts
¼ pound lean beef
3 green onions
2 tablespoons cooking oil
1 (10½-oz.) can beef broth or 2 cups bouillon
2 tablespoons soy sauce

Slice beef into small, very thin pieces. Chop fine the white part of the green onions, reserving the green tops. Sauté meat and onion in cooking oil until meat is well seared—about 5 minutes. Add sprouts, broth or bouillon and soy sauce. Simmer covered about 20 minutes, or until meat is tender, but not until the sprouts become soggy. Five minutes before serving, add the green onion tops, cut into ½-inch lengths.

Sparerib and Sprout Soup

(2 to 4 Servings)

A hearty cold-weather soup.

2 cups Soybean Sprouts
1 pound spareribs
2 tablespoons cooking oil
1 medium-size onion
3 cups bouillon or water
½ teaspoon salt
pinch of pepper

Have butcher cut spareribs into 2-inch pieces. Brown the ribs in the cooking oil. Chop onion fine and add to spareribs. Cook until onions are translucent. Add bouillon or water, salt and pepper and cook covered for 20 minutes. Add sprouts and cook until they are tender—about 20 additional minutes.

Chicken and Sprout Soup

(2 to 4 Servings)

1 cup Mung Bean Sprouts
1 pound chicken wings
3 cups chicken broth or water
1 teaspoon salt
1 small onion
2 tablespoons cooking oil
pinch of powdered ginger
1 hard-boiled egg
1 tablespoon chopped parsley

Put chicken wings, salt and chicken broth or water in pan and cook covered until chicken is tender—about 30 minutes. Remove meat from bones and return to the broth. Chop onion fine and sauté in the cooking oil until translucent and slightly brown. Add onion, powdered ginger and sprouts to broth. Cook until sprouts are just tender—approximately 15 to 20 minutes. Slice egg and float slices on top of soup; garnish with chopped parsley.

Egg and Sprout Soup

(2 to 4 Servings)

2 cups sprouts
3 cups chicken or beef broth
salt and pepper to taste
1 egg
1 tablespoon chopped parsley

Heat broth. Add sprouts—Mung Bean, Soybean, Wheat or Rice, all are good. Cook covered until sprouts are tender—12 to 30 minutes, depending on the kind used. Season to taste and remove from heat. In a small bowl, beat egg until frothy and quickly stir into the hot broth with a fork. Garnish with parsley and serve immediately.

Variation: before stirring in the beaten egg, add up to a cup of cooked noodles, spaghetti or vermicelli.

Green Pea Sprout Soup

(2 to 4 Servings)

Served with *Sprouted Wheat Bread*, this can make a hearty, whole cold-weather meal.

2 cups Green Pea Sprouts
1 medium onion, chopped
1 slice Canadian bacon, chopped
3 cups meat stock or water
1 medium potato, diced
2 carrots, chopped
salt and pepper to taste

Cook onion and Canadian bacon in a heavy pan until onion is translucent. Add meat stock or water, sprouts, carrots and potato. Cook covered slowly for 30 to 40 minutes. Season to taste.

Vegetarian Sprout Soup

(2 or 3 Servings)

1 cup Soybean Sprouts
1 small onion
2 tablespoons cooking oil
½ cup chopped celery
¼ cup chopped carrot
2 tablespoons vegetable flakes
3 cups vegetable stock or water
1 cup peas, fresh or canned
salt and pepper to taste
parsley or chives

Sauté onion in cooking oil until golden brown. Put sprouts, celery, carrots and vegetable flakes in vegetable stock or water. Add sauteed onion and simmer covered until sprouts are tender—about 30 minutes. Add peas, salt, pepper and cook 3 or 4 minutes more. Serve with parsley or chive garnish.

Navy Bean Soup

(2 or 3 Servings)

2 cups Navy (or Pea) Bean Sprouts
1 medium onion, chopped
2 tablespoons butter
3 cups vegetable or meat stock
¼ teaspoon celery salt
½ teaspoon salt
pepper to taste

Sauté onion in butter. Add remaining ingredients. Cook covered slowly for 20 to 30 minutes. If desired, the mixture can be blended until smooth and returned to pan long enough to bring soup to boiling point. Garnish with chopped parsley, chives or watercress.

Squash and Millet Soup

(2 or 3 Servings)

1 cup Millet (or Rye) Sprouts
1 tablespoon cooking oil
2 tablespoons chopped onion
2½ cups vegetable stock or water
½ cup summer squash, cubed
2 teaspoons soy sauce
1 tablespoon chopped parsley

Sauté onion in cooking oil until translucent. Add stock or water and sprouts and cook covered for 15 minutes. Add squash and soy sauce. Cook for 10 minutes more. Serve with parsley garnish.

Potato and Sprout Soup

(2 or 3 Servings)

1 cup Fenugreek Sprouts
1 medium potato
2 tablespoons chopped onion
1 tablespoon butter
1 cup vegetable stock or water

1 cup milk or light cream
salt to taste

Cook potato in skin until just tender; peal, dice and set aside. Sauté onion in butter. Add vegetable stock or water, sprouts and diced potato. Cook covered for 10 to 15 minutes. Add milk or light cream and bring just to boil. Salt to taste and serve with chopped parsley or chive garnish.

Tomato and Rice Sprout Soup

(2 to 4 Servings)

1 cup Brown Rice Sprouts
4 large fresh tomatoes or 1 (16-oz.) can
1 cup meat stock or water
1 small onion, chopped
¾ teaspoon salt
½ bay leaf

If fresh tomatoes are used, peal and cut into small pieces. Put tomatoes, stock or water, onion, sprouts, salt and bay leaf into saucepan and simmer covered slowly until sprouts are just tender—about 30 minutes. Remove bay leaf and serve garnished with grated cheese or chopped parsley.

Asparagus and Sprout Soup

(2 to 4 Servings)

1 cup Mung Bean Sprouts
1 (10½-oz.) can cream of chicken soup
1 cup milk or light cream
1 cup cooked asparagus
salt and pepper to taste
1 hard-boiled egg
2 tablespoons chopped parsley

Put chicken soup and milk or light cream in saucepan and mix thoroughly. Add cooked asparagus (either canned or left-over fresh will do) and sprouts. Simmer covered for 10 to 15 minutes. Season to taste and garnish with parsley and finely chopped hard-boiled egg.

Corn and Mung Bean Soup

(2 to 4 Servings)

This a dandy vegetarian soup.

1½ cups Mung Bean Sprouts
1 tablespoon melted butter or cooking oil
1 tablespoon cornstarch
3 cups vegetable stock or water
1 tablespoon soy sauce
1 cup cooked corn
1 small onion, chopped
salt and pepper to taste

Heat butter or cooking oil in pan. Add cornstarch, stirring until smooth. Cook for 2 or 3 minutes. Gradually add vegetable stock or water, soy sauce, cooked corn, chopped onion and sprouts. Simmer covered until sprouts are done—about 10 or 12 minutes. Salt and pepper to taste.

Corn Sprout Chowder

(2 to 4 Servings)

1½ cups Corn Sprouts
3 strips bacon, diced fine
1 medium onion, diced fine
1 cup diced raw potato
1 cup water
2 cups milk
salt and pepper to taste
chopped parsley garnish

Cook diced bacon gently in frying pan until done but not crisp; drain off fat. Add diced onion and cook until translucent but not brown. Put onion, bacon, sprouts, potato and water in saucepan and cook until sprouts and potato are tender but not mushy. Add milk and seasonings. Heat almost to boiling point, garnish with parsley and serve immediately.

Soybean Soup

(2 or 3 Servings)

1 cup Soybean Sprouts
2 cups water
1 small onion, minced
½ cup chopped celery
½ cup chopped carrots
2 teaspoons vegetable flakes
1 teaspoon salt
2 teaspoons chopped parsley

Chop or grind the sprouts coarsely. Combine all ingredients except the parsley in saucepan. Cover and cook slowly for 20 minutes. Serve garnished with parsley.

Variation: for a heartier soup, meat stock can be substituted for the water and small pieces of leftover meat added.

Kidney Bean Soup

(2 or 3 Servings)

2 cups Kidney Bean Sprouts
1 small onion, chopped
2 tablespoons cooking oil
1 teaspoon oregano
½ teaspoon celery salt
1 teaspoon salt
2 cups meat stock, bouillon or water
lemon slices

Sauté onion in cooking oil. Add remaining ingredients except lemon slices. Cook covered for about 30 minutes or until sprouts are tender. Pour into blender and blend until smooth. Return to saucepan and bring to boil. Serve in individual bowls topped with a slice of lemon.

Buckwheat Soup

(2 or 3 Servings)

1 cup Buckwheat Sprouts
1 tablespoon butter
2 tablespoons chopped onion
1 cup water
2 cups milk
½ teaspoon salt
2 tablespoons chopped parsley or watercress

Sauté onions in butter until golden brown. Add sprouts, water, milk and salt. Cook covered over low heat for 10 to 15 minutes. Garnish with parsley or watercress.

salads

Here are six tasty and filling full-meal salads to try.

Ham and Sprout Salad

(2 to 4 Servings)

A fine way to use leftover ham—in whatever amount you have.

2 cups Mung Bean Sprouts
¾ cup (or more) ham, chopped
2 stalks celery, diced
2 scallions, chopped
1 hard-boiled egg, sliced
¼ cup cooked water chestnuts
dressing of choice

Combine all ingredients and chill thoroughly. Dress just before serving.
Variation ideas: substitute other sprouts or use any other kind of leftover cold meat, fish or chicken—the results will be equally delicious.

Seafood and Sprout Salad

(2 to 4 Servings)

This is a highly nutritious dieter's delight for a satisfying meal any time of year.

2 cups Mung Bean Sprouts
2 scallions, chopped
2/3 cup shrimp or crab meat pieces
½ cup yogurt
1 tablespoon lemon juice
1 tablespoon soy sauce
¼ teaspoon salt
pinch of curry powder
pinch of garlic powder
2 or 3 sprigs fresh parsley for garnish

Combine sprouts, scallions and shrimp or crab meat. In a small bowl mix together the yogurt, lemon juice, soy sauce and seasonings. Pour dressing over the sprout mixture. Serve well chilled on beds of salad greens, garnished with parsley.

Artichoke and Egg Salad

(2 or 3 Servings)

1 cup Mung Bean Sprouts
6 to 8 cooked artichoke hearts, sliced
1/3 cup shredded raw carrot
1/3 cup shredded Swiss cheese
3 strips bacon, fried crisp and crumbled
2 hard-boiled eggs, sliced
dressing of choice

Combine all ingredients, toss thoroughly and serve chilled. Salad may be served on beds of salad greens or just as is.

Note: hold back on adding the dressing and salad may be kept in the refrigerator for several hours before serving.

Four-Sprout Julienne Salad

(2 to 4 Servings)

½ cup Alfalfa Sprouts
½ cup Mung Bean Sprouts
½ cup Adzuki Bean Sprouts
½ cup Cabbage Sprouts
shredded salad greens
¼ cup diced celery
¼ cup diced cucumber
¼ cup julienne strips ham
¼ cup julienne strips chicken
¼ cup julienne strips Swiss or Cheddar cheese
1 hard-boiled egg, sliced
2/3 cup dressing of choice

Arrange shredded salad greens in salad bowl. Add other ingredients in successive layers, pouring the dressing over the mixture just before serving. Toss lightly and serve with one of the sprout quick-breads or rolls.

Three-Bean and Sprout Salad

(2 to 4 Servings)

1½ cups Mung Bean Sprouts
½ cup cooked wax beans
½ cup cooked green beans
½ cup cooked lima or kidney beans
½ green pepper, cut in strips
1 small onion, thinly sliced
2/3 cup leftover meat, cubed
¼ cup blue cheese, crumbled
dressing of choice

Combine all ingredients and chill thoroughly before serving.
Variation: other sprouts may be substituted for the Mung Bean sprouts. Experiment until you find your favorite combination.

Chicken and Sprout Salad

(2 to 4 Servings)

½ cup Mung Bean Sprouts
1½ cups Rice Sprouts
1 cup cooked chicken breast, shredded
2 tablespoons chopped scallion or chives

Dressing:

2 tablespoons sesame or safflower oil
1 tablespoon soy sauce
1 tablespoon wine vinegar
¼ teaspoon salt
¼ teaspoon celery salt
½ teaspoon sugar
pinch of pepper

Combine sprouts, chicken and scallion or chives. Chill thoroughly. Meanwhile make dressing by combining all ingredients in bowl or glass jar. Just before serving pour dressing over chicken-sprout mixture and toss lightly. Serve on bed of salad greens.

The following make excellent side-dish salads.

Mixed Sprout Slaw

(2 to 4 Servings)

This is a good way to use up small amounts of different sprouts—the more kinds the better.

1 to 2 cups sprouts
1 large carrot, grated or shredded
½ cup diced celery
1 tablespoon finely minced onion
1 tablespoon minced parsley
¼ cup currants or chopped raisins
1/3 cup mayonnaise

Combine all ingredients and serve on beds of salad greens.

Basic Sprout Salad

(2 Servings)

 1 cup Mung Bean Sprouts
 1 cup salad greens
 dressing of choice

Start with sprouts and salad greens; add whatever else is at hand or that appeals—broccoli, cabbage, carrot, cauliflower, celery, chive, cucumber, mushroom, olive, onion, pickle, pimiento, pepper, radish, scallion, tomato and finely shredded meat or seafood are ideas. Any prepared dressing may be used: try Italian one time and French the next. Better yet, try one of the dressings given here or make your own preservative-free favorite.

Calorie-Counter's Dressing

(1 Serving)

 1 tablespoon soy sauce
 2 teaspoons vegetable oil
 2 teaspoons water
 salt, pepper and onion or garlic powder to taste

Blend all ingredients and refrigerate until ready to serve.
 Variation: add 1 teaspoon shredded pickled ginger.

Yogurt Dressing

(1 Cup)

 ¾ cup plain yogurt
 ¼ cup mayonnaise
 1 tablespoon minced onion
 ½ teaspoon salt
 pinch each pepper, mustard and curry powder

Mix well and refrigerate before serving.

Sour Cream Dressing

(1 Cup)

1 cup sour cream
4 tablespoons chopped chives
3 tablespoons lemon juice
½ teaspoon salt

Blend thoroughly and chill before serving.

Wheat Sprout Salad

(2 to 4 Servings)

1½ cups barely sprouted Wheat Sprouts
½ cup cottage cheese
3 or 4 radishes, finely chopped
1 tablespoon minced onion
2 tablespoons chopped parsley
salt and pepper to taste
¼ cup yogurt or sour cream

Combine sprouts, cottage cheese, radishes, onion, parsley and seasonings. Mix gently and chill. Serve with yogurt or sour cream drizzled over the salad. Garnish with dusting of paprika.

Cucumber and Sprout Salad

(2 to 4 Servings)

1 cup Mung Bean or Soybean Sprouts
½ cup watercress or lettuce, shredded
1 cucumber, diced
½ cup Swiss cheese, diced
10 pitted ripe olives, chopped coarsely
dressing of choice

Combine all ingredients and serve immediately.

Tomato and Alfalfa Sprout Salad

(2 to 4 Servings)

    1 cup Alfalfa Sprouts
    2 tomatoes, sliced
    1 cucumber, sliced thin
    dressing of choice
    salad greens

Combine sprouts, tomatoes and cucumbers. Add dressing and toss to mix. Refrigerate for several hours. Serve ice cold on salad greens.

    Variation idea: just before serving, add ¼ cup grated cheese or seasoned bread crumbs.

Cabbage and Sprout Slaw

(2 to 4 Servings)

This has particular eye appeal if red cabbage is used.

    1 cup Mung Bean Sprouts
    1 cup cabbage, shredded
    1 cup lettuce, shredded
    3 tablespoons minced onion
    ½ teaspoon celery seed
    2/3 cup *Sour Cream* or *Yogurt Dressing*

Combine all ingredients and serve cold.

Mushroom and Sprout Salad

(2 or 3 Servings)

    1½ cups Mung Bean Sprouts
    ½ cup sliced mushrooms
    2 tablespoons vegetable oil
    1 cup spinach or lettuce, shredded
    2 tablespoons minced scallion or chives
    dressing of choice or *Calorie-Counter's Dressing*

Sauté mushrooms in oil until golden brown. Let cool. Combine sprouts, spinach or lettuce and scallions or chives. Add cooled mushrooms and dressing. Toss lightly and serve cool.

Shrimp and Bean Sprout Salad

(2 to 4 Servings)

1 cup Mung Bean Sprouts
1 cup cabbage, shredded fine
½ cup cooked shrimp, shredded
   or use tiny whole ones
2 tablespoons minced scallions
1 small cucumber, sliced thin
¼ cup lemon juice
1 tablespoon salad oil
1 tablespoon soy sauce
1 tablespoon sugar

Combine sprouts, cabbage, shrimp, scallions and cucumber. In a small bowl combine remaining ingredients. Pour over shrimp and sprout mixture, mix well and serve on bed of salad greens. Just before serving sprinkle with a dash of paprika.

Chickpea Sprout Salad

(2 or 3 Servings)

1½ cups Chick-Pea Sprouts
1 tomato, diced
¼ cup minced scallions or chives
¼ cup minced parsley
¼ cup salad oil
2 tablespoons vinegar or lemon juice
salt and pepper to taste

Combine sprouts, tomato, scallions or chives and parsley. In a small bowl combine other ingredients. Add to salad and toss well.

Watercress and Sprout Salad

(2 or 3 Servings)

The watercress lends a spicy touch that makes this salad particularly good with lamb or chicken dishes.

    1½ cups Mung Bean Sprouts
    1 bunch watercress
    1 tablespoon minced chives
    2 tablespoons salad oil
    1 tablespoon vinegar
    1 tablespoon soy sauce
    1 teaspoon sugar

Combine sprouts, watercress and chives. Chill in refrigerator for a few hours. In small bowl mix oil, vinegar, soy sauce and sugar. Just before serving pour dressing over sprout-watercress mixture.

Wheat Sprout Taboulleh Salad

(2 to 4 Servings)

A tangy combination of flavors that goes especially well with somewhat bland fish, poultry or egg dishes.

    1½ cups barely sprouted Wheat Sprouts
    ½ cup finely chopped parsley
    2 tablespoons minced onion
    1 small cucumber, diced fine
    ½ green pepper, diced fine
    ¼ cup finely chopped celery
    ¼ cup salad oil
    ¼ cup lemon juice
    salt and pepper to taste

In a glass or ceramic bowl combine sprouts and all vegetables. In a small bowl mix oil, lemon juice, salt and pepper. Pour dressing over sprout mixture and blend well. Refrigerate for several hours or overnight. Serve cold garnished with salad greens.

Rice Sprout Salad

(2 to 4 Servings)

1 cup Rice Sprouts
1 cup Mung Bean or Soybean Sprouts
1 small onion, sliced thin
¼ cup chopped pimiento
¼ cup chopped green pepper
¼ cup diced celery
¼ cup salad oil
¼ cup vinegar
1 teaspoon sugar
½ teaspoon salt
pinch of pepper

Combine sprouts, onion, pimiento, green pepper and celery. In a small bowl mix oil, vinegar, sugar, salt and pepper. Add dressing to sprout mixture, toss lightly and serve chilled.

Avocado-Sprout Salad

(2 to 4 Servings)

1 cup Mung Bean Sprouts
1 cup lettuce, shredded
1 avocado, cubed
1 medium onion, sliced thin
3 or 4 strips pimiento, diced
¼ cup vegetable oil
2 tablespoons lemon juice or vinegar
pinch of sugar or speck of honey
pinch of dry mustard
salt and pepper to taste

Combine sprouts, lettuce, avocado, onion and pimiento and chill. In small bowl mix remaining ingredients and sprinkle over sprout mixture. Serve immediately and ice cold.

Cheese and Sprout Salad

(2 to 4 Servings)

1½ cups Mung Bean or Soybean Sprouts
1 tomato, cubed
¼ cup green pepper, chopped
¼ cup minced onion or scallions
2 tablespoons parsley, chopped
1/3 cup cheese, grated or shredded
dressing of choice or
   ½ cup *Sour Cream Dressing*

Combine sprouts, tomato, pepper, onions or scallions, parsley and cheese. Mix thoroughly. Drizzle dressing over the salad just before serving.

Cottage Cheese and Sprout Tomatoes

(2 Servings)

2/3 cup Mung Bean Sprouts
2/3 cup cottage cheese
3 tablespoons chopped scallions or chives
salt to taste
2 large tomatoes
1 teaspoon chopped parsley

Combine sprouts, cottage cheese, scallions or chives and salt. Slice top off tomatoes, remove seeds and center pulp. Stuff tomatoes with sprout and cheese mixture. Sprinkle parsley on top and serve cold.

Fruit and Sprout Salad

(2 to 4 Servings)

1 cup Mung Bean or Soy Sprouts
1 apple, sliced thin
2 bananas, sliced
2 or 3 tablespoons orange or lemon juice
¼ cup chopped dates
¼ cup chopped nuts
1/3 cup mayonnaise or yogurt

Sprinkle orange or lemon juice over apple and banana to keep from darkening. Add sprouts, dates, nuts and mayonnaise or yogurt. Serve on bed of salad greens and sprinkle a bit of cinnamon on each serving.

Apple-Sprout Salad

(2 to 4 Servings)

1 cup Mung Bean Sprouts
1 cup cabbage, shredded
1 apple, chopped
¼ cup currants or raisins
¼ cup sour cream
2 tablespoons tarragon vinegar
1 tablespoon sugar
¼ teaspoon salt

Combine sprouts, cabbage, apple and currants or raisins. In a small bowl mix sour cream, vinegar, sugar and salt. Pour dressing over salad and toss lightly. Serve on crisp salad greens.

Variation idea: substitute Mustard, Radish or Alfalfa Sprouts for the Mung Bean Sprouts.

Molded Sprout Salad

(4 to 6 Servings)

1 cup Mung Bean Sprouts
1 package lemon or lime gelatin
1½ cups hot water
4 tablespoons lemon juice
pinch of salt
1 cup finely shredded cabbage
½ cup shredded carrots
¼ cup minced celery
1 tablespoon minced chives or onion

Dissolve gelatin in hot water. Add lemon juice and salt. Cool until partly thickened. Add remaining ingredients and mix well. Pour into mold and chill until completely set. Unmold and serve with mayonnaise or *Sour Cream Dressing* on a bed of salad greens.

Molded Fruit and Sprout Salad

(4 to 6 Servings)

1 cup Mung Bean Sprouts
1 envelope unflavored gelatin
½ cup cold water
½ cup boiling water
¾ cup fruit juice
¼ cup lemon juice
1 cup sliced fruit—peaches, pineapple, grapefruit
   or orange
½ cup shredded coconut or chopped apple

Sprinkle gelatin on cold water to soften. Soon after add boiling water and stir until dissolved. Add fruit juice (if canned fruits are used, that juice may be included), lemon juice and the fruits. Stir well, pour into mold and put in refrigerator to cool. Stir once when mixture has begun to set. When set, unmold and serve with mayonnaise, *Sour Cream Dressing* or *Yogurt Dressing* on a bed of greens.

Shrimp Sprout Aspic

(4 to 6 Servings)

1 cup Mung Bean Sprouts
1 envelope unflavored gelatin
¼ cup cold water
½ cup boiling water
1 cup tomato sauce
¼ cup lemon juice
½ cup diced celery
1 tablespoon minced onion
1 cup shrimp, shredded

Sprinkle gelatin on cold water to soften. Add boiling water and stir until dissolved. Add tomato sauce and lemon juice. Mix well and refrigerate until partly set. Add celery, onion and shrimp. Blend thoroughly and pour into mold. Refrigerate until completely set. Serve on bed of salad greens with mayonnaise, *Sour Cream Dressing* or *Yogurt Dressing.*

main dishes

Beef with Mung Bean Sprouts

(2 to 4 Servings)

2½ cups Mung Bean Sprouts
2 tablespoons peanut, safflower or corn oil
½ pound lean beefsteak (tenderloin or round)
½ cup celery, shredded
2 tablespoons onion or scallion, minced
2 tablespoons soy sauce
dash of cooking sherry
salt and pepper to taste

Cut beef into 1-inch strips and slice very thin across grain. Heat oil in wok or heavy frying pan. Add meat and stir-fry for 3 or 4 minutes. Add celery and onion. Stir-fry for 1 minute. Add sprouts and seasonings. Stir-fry for another 1 or 2 minutes. Cover and cook for about 5 minutes —until the bean sprouts are just translucent. Serve with brown rice and a salad.

Beef and Rice Sprouts

(2 to 4 Servings)

This is a much heartier dish than the *Beef with Mung Bean Sprouts.*

2 cups barely sprouted Rice Sprouts
¼ cup beef broth or bouillon
1 tablespoon soy sauce
2 teaspoons cornstarch
pinch of sugar
2 tablespoons peanut, safflower or corn oil

½ pound lean beefsteak (tenderloin or round)
1 small onion or 3 scallions, chopped
¼ green pepper, chopped

In a small bowl combine broth or bouillon, soy sauce, cornstarch and sugar. Set mixture aside. Cut beef into 1-inch strips and slice thin across the grain. Heat oil in wok or frying pan and add beef. Stir-fry until meat just changes color. Add sprouts, onion or scallions and pepper. Stir-fry for 2 or 3 minutes. Cover and cook for 3 minutes. Add cornstarch mixture and stir well. Cover and cook for another 2 minutes.

Variation idea: add 2 tablespoons shredded pickled ginger or chopped sweet pickles.

Soy Sprout Meat Loaf

(4 to 6 Servings)

This is just as good cold as it is hot, and makes fine sandwiches.

1½ cups Soybean Sprouts, coarsely ground
1½ pounds ground meat (beef, pork and veal or lamb mix)
1 medium onion, chopped fine
¼ cup bread crumbs
¼ cup wheat germ
1 egg, well beaten
2 tablespoons chopped parsley
1 teaspoon salt
pinch of pepper
milk as needed

In a large bowl combine all ingredients, using as much milk as necessary to make a soft (but not sloppy) mixture. Pack mixture into lightly greased loaf pan. Bake in 350 oven for about an hour—until meat is browned on top and has started to pull away from the edges of the pan. Serve garnished with parsley sprays or cheese sauce.

Variation: try any of your favorite sprouts in this fine meat loaf recipe.

Sweet and Sour Beef With Bean Sprouts

(2 to 4 Servings)

2 cups Mung Bean Sprouts
¼ cup cider vinegar
2 tablespoons water
3 tablespoons cornstarch
1/3 cup brown sugar
1 tablespoon soy sauce
2 tablespoons peanut, safflower or corn oil
½ pound lean beefsteak (tenderloin or round), sliced thin
4 scallions, sliced in 1-inch lengths
½ cup water chestnuts, sliced
6 radishes, sliced thin

Combine vinegar, water, cornstarch, sugar and soy sauce. Set mixture aside. Heat oil in wok or heavy frying pan. Add meat and stir-fry for 2 minutes. Remove meat from pan. Put scallions, water chestnuts and radishes in pan. Stir-fry for 1 or 2 minutes. Add sauce and cook for another 1 or 2 minutes. Add bean sprouts and cook covered for 5 minutes. Add partially cooked meat and cook 1 more minute. Serve with rice and noodles.

Calorie Counter's Spaghetti

(2 Servings)

Anyone who is trying to limit food intake will appreciate this rich tasting—but low calorie—dish. The sprouts give it an added appeal that is very pleasant.

3 to 4 cups Mung Bean Sprouts
1 to 2 cups favorite spaghetti sauce, heated
grated cheese (optional)

Steam sprouts for 4 or 5 minutes—they should be just translucent, but not soft. Pour hot sauce over the drained sprouts and top with grated cheese, if desired. Serve with a crisp green salad.

Sprout Stuffed Zucchini

(2 to 4 Servings)

1½ cups cooked Rice Sprouts
1 zucchini, 8 or 9 inches long
¾ pound ground beef
¼ cup chopped onion
2 stalks celery, chopped
2 tablespoons minced parsley
1 teaspoon salt
¼ teaspoon oregano
pinch of pepper
¾ cup tomato sauce or undiluted tomato soup

To cook sprouts, simmer in water for 5 to 8 minutes or steam for 10. While sprouts cook, pan-fry ground beef until about two-thirds done and drain to remove excess fat. Cut slice from each end of zucchini. Scoop out center seeds and pulp and discard. Add cooked sprouts, onion, celery, parsley and seasonings to drained meat. Stuff zucchini with mixture and place in greased loaf pan. Pour tomato sauce or soup over the zucchini. Bake at 350 for 45 to 60 minutes. Zucchini should be tender when pricked with fork, but not soft. Serve with additional hot sauce, if desired.

Spiced Beef and Bean Sprouts

(2 to 4 Servings)

2 cups Mung Bean Sprouts
1 tablespoon vegetable oil
1 tablespoon soy sauce
¼ teaspoon Tabasco sauce
pinch of salt
pinch of powdered ginger
½ pound lean beefsteak (tenderloin or round)
2 tablespoons peanut, safflower or corn oil
3 scallions, cut in short lengths

½ cup mushrooms, sliced thin
¾ cup snow peas, shredded
¼ cup beef broth or bouillon
1 tablespoon cornstarch

In a shallow bowl combine vegetable oil, soy sauce, Tabasco sauce, salt and ginger. Cut beef into 1-inch wide strips and slice very thin across the grain. Put sliced beef in the soy sauce marinade, let sit for 1 hour and drain. Heat the 2 tablespoons of peanut, safflower or corn oil in wok or heavy frying pan. Stir-fry the drained meat for 2 minutes and remove from pan. Put scallions, mushrooms and snow peas in the pan. Stir-fry for 1 or 2 minutes. Add sprouts and stir-fry for 3 or 4 minutes. Add partially cooked meat and cook, covered, for another 3 or 4 minutes. Meanwhile combine the beef broth or bouillon and cornstarch. Add to the meat-sprouts mixture and blend well, cooking another 1 or 2 minutes. Serve with noodles or rice.

Veal and Sprouts

(2 or 3 Servings)

3 cups Mung Bean Sprouts
2 tablespoons corn, safflower or peanut oil
3 scallions or 1 small onion, sliced thin
1 cup lean veal, shredded thin
¼ cup celery, shredded
2 tablespoons soy sauce
1 tablespoon water
2 tablespoons dry sherry wine
1 tablespoon cornstarch
¼ teaspoon ginger
salt and pepper to taste

Heat oil in wok or heavy frying pan. Add scallions or onion and stir-fry for 2 or 3 minutes. Add veal and stir-fry until color changes. Add sprouts and celery. Combine soy sauce, water, wine, cornstarch, ginger, salt and pepper. Add to meat and vegetable mixture. Cook over high heat until juice thickens. Serve piping hot with rice or noodles.

Pork With Bean Sprouts

(2 to 4 Servings)

This is a good basic recipe, but any number of different ingredients may be added—mushrooms, water chestnuts, celery, snow peas, green peas or pickled ginger, to name only a few.

> 3 cups Mung Bean Sprouts
> 2 tablespoons peanut, safflower or corn oil
> 1 small onion, sliced thin
> 1 cup lean pork, shredded thin
> 2 tablespoons soy sauce
> 2 tablespoons chicken or beef broth
> 1 teaspoon vinegar
> pinch of salt
> ½ teaspoon sugar
> 2 tablespoons chopped parsley

Heat oil in heavy frying pan or wok. Add onion and stir-fry for 2 or 3 minutes. Add pork and stir-fry until meat changes color. Combine soy sauce, broth, vinegar, salt and sugar. Pour over meat and onion. Bring to bubbling hot. Add sprouts and mix well. Cook covered for 3 to 5 minutes. Remove from heat and add parsley. Serve immediately with rice or noodles.

Spicy Hot Pork

(2 to 4 Servings)

> 3 cups Soybean Sprouts
> 3 tablespoons peanut, safflower or corn oil
> 1 clove garlic, minced (optional)
> 1 small onion, diced
> 1 cup lean pork, shredded thin
> ¼ cup hot peppers, shredded thin
> 3 tablespoons soy sauce
> 2 tablespoons dry sherry wine
> 1 teaspoon vinegar

1 teaspoon sugar
pinch of ginger
pinch of pepper
pinch of salt

Heat oil in heavy frying pan or wok. Add garlic, onion, pork and peppers. Stir-fry for 3 or 4 minutes, until pork has changed color. Combine soy sauce, wine, vinegar, sugar, ginger, pepper and salt. Pour over meat mixture. Add sprouts and mix well. Cook covered for 8 to 10 minutes—sprouts should be tender but not soft. Serve with plain boiled rice and watch out—this is hot!

Chinese Chicken and Bean Sprouts

(2 to 4 Servings)

This is the basic traditional Chinese way of preparing chicken and bean sprouts. No two cooks ever do it exactly the same way, so feel free to experiment with your own ideas.

2 cups Mung Bean Sprouts
3 tablespoons peanut, safflower or corn oil
1 to 2 cups cooked chicken, shredded
¼ cup minced onion or scallions
½ cup mushrooms, sliced thin
½ green pepper, sliced thin
½ cup celery, shredded thin
¾ cup chicken broth or bouillon
¼ cup water
2 tablespoons soy sauce
2 tablespoons cornstarch

Heat oil in wok or heavy frying pan. Add chicken and stir-fry for 1 or 2 minutes. Add onion or scallions, mushrooms, green pepper and celery. Stir-fry for 3 or 4 minutes. Add sprouts and chicken broth or bouillon. Simmer covered for 3 minutes. Combine water, soy sauce and cornstarch. Add to chicken-sprout mixture in frying pan. Cook until the broth thickens slightly. Serve immediately with rice or noodles.

Baked Chicken

(2 to 4 Servings)

This is a marvelously tasty way to do chicken that is both nutritious and fat-free.

1 cup Soybean, Wheat or Rice Sprouts, oven-dried
   and ground
1 egg
2 tablespoons milk
1 teaspoon salt
1 broiling chicken, quartered

Roast the ground sprouts on a cookie sheet in 300 oven, stirring occasionally, until golden brown—about 15 minutes. When sprouts have cooled, put in shallow dish. Meanwhile combine egg, milk and salt in bowl and beat well. Dip each piece of chicken in egg mixture then roll in roasted sprouts. Lay coated chicken on lightly greased baking pan or dish. Bake at 350 for about 1 hour, or until tender.

Chicken cooked this way is equally good hot or cold.

Chicken Livers and Bean Sprouts

(2 or 3 Servings)

1½ cups Mung Bean Sprouts
2 tablespoons peanut, safflower or corn oil
1 small onion, sliced thin
¾ pound chicken livers, cut in bite-size pieces
1 tablespoon soy sauce
1 tablespoon dry sherry
salt and pepper to taste

Heat oil in heavy frying pan or wok. Add onion and stir-fry for 2 minutes. Add chicken livers and stir-fry for 2 or 3 minutes—until partly cooked. Add sprouts, soy sauce and sherry. Cook covered for 5 minutes. Season with salt and pepper to taste and serve piping hot with rice or cooked noodles and a salad.

Creamed Chicken With Sprouts

(2 to 4 Servings)

The sprouts give this quick and easy dish a nice texture.

1½ cups Mung Bean Sprouts
1 (10½-oz.) can cream of mushroom soup
½ cup milk or light cream
1 tablespoon minced onion
1 cup cooked green peas
1½ cups cooked chicken, diced
salt and pepper to taste

Put soup in saucepan or double boiler. Add milk and stir until blended. Add other ingredients and cook over low heat for 5 to 10 minutes. Serve on toast, rice or cooked noodles.

Turkey With Bean Sprouts

(2 to 4 Servings)

This is a fine way to use up leftover holiday turkey. The amount of turkey can vary, depending on how much you have on hand.

2 cups Mung Bean Sprouts
3 tablespoons peanut, safflower or corn oil
2 cups cooked turkey, sliced thin and shredded
2 tablespoons soy sauce
1 tablespoon dry sherry wine
pinch each of salt, pepper and sugar

Heat oil in heavy frying pan or wok. Add shredded turkey. Stir-fry for 1 minute. Add sprouts and stir-fry for another 1 or 2 minutes. Add soy sauce, sherry and seasonings. Cook covered for about 2 minutes. Serve piping hot with cooked Rice or Wheat Sprouts and a crisp green salad.

Variation idea: if you have only a small amount of turkey and/or you want greater nutrition, use Soybean Sprouts and increase the covered cooking time to about 10 minutes.

Sprout Stuffed Rock Cornish Hen

(2 Servings)

1 cup barely sprouted Rice Sprouts
1 stalk celery, diced fine
1 tablespoon minced onion
1 tablespoon minced parsley
½ teaspoon salt
½ teaspoon grated lemon or orange peel
pinch of pepper
2 Rock Cornish hens
2 tablespoons melted butter or margarine
2 tablespoons soy sauce
2 tablespoons softened orange marmalade

If frozen, first thaw hens. Then combine sprouts, celery, onion, parsley, salt, lemon or orange peel and pepper. Stuff hens with mixture. Bake on greased pan according to package directions for hens. As hens bake, brush 3 or 4 times with mixture of melted butter or margarine, soy sauce and marmalade.

Lamb With Peas

(2 to 4 Servings)

3 cups Pea Sprouts
2 tablespoons peanut, safflower or corn oil
1 garlic clove, minced (optional)
1 small onion, diced
1½ cups lamb, shredded thin
¼ cup celery, shredded
3 tablespoons soy sauce
¼ cup chicken broth or bouillon
½ bay leaf
pinch of salt

Heat oil in heavy frying pan or wok. Add garlic and onion. Stir-fry for 3 or 4 minutes. Add lamb and stir-fry for 2 more minutes. Add sprouts, celery, soy sauce, broth or bouillon, bay leaf and salt. Cook covered for 5 or 6 minutes. Remove bay leaf and serve piping hot.

Fish With Bean Sprouts

(2 to 4 Servings)

3 cups Mung Bean Sprouts
½ cup water
½ to ¾ pound fresh fish (sea bass, sole or
    flounder), cut in chunks
1 teaspoon salt
2 tablespoons peanut, safflower or corn oil
4 tablespoons minced onion
3 tablespoons soy sauce
1 tablespoon dry sherry wine
pinch of ginger

Put water in saucepan and add fish and salt. Cook covered over slow heat until fish will flake readily. Set drained and flaked fish aside. Heat oil in heavy frying pan or wok. Add onion and stir-fry until translucent. Add soy sauce, wine and ginger. Bring to boil. Add flaked fish and sprouts. Heat quickly to boil and serve immediately over rice or noodles.

Crab With Bean Sprouts

(2 or 3 Servings)

Frozen king crab meat is particularly good in this dish.

3 cups Mung Bean Sprouts
3 tablespoons peanut, safflower or corn oil
1 small onion or 3 scallions, sliced thin
½ cup mushroom, sliced
2 tablespoons minced parsley
½ cup celery, shredded
4 tablespoons soy sauce
2 tablespoons dry sherry wine
1 teaspoon sugar
½ teaspoon salt
1 cup crab meat, cooked and shredded

Heat oil in heavy frying pan or wok. Add onion or scallions. Stir-fry for 2 minutes. Add sprouts, mushroom, parsley and celery. Stir-fry for another 1 or 2 minutes. In a small bowl combine soy sauce, wine, sugar and salt. Add crab to sprout mixture. Mix well and stir-fry for 2 or 3 minutes. Add soy sauce mixture and bring to bubbling hot. Serve immediately over rice or noodles.

Shrimp and Wheat Berries

(2 to 4 Servings)

A rich and highly nutritious dish with a piquant flavor all its own.

2½ cups barely sprouted Wheat Sprouts
¾ cup Mung Bean Sprouts
3 tablespoons peanut, safflower or corn oil
1 small onion, chopped
1 garlic clove, minced (optional)
1 cup shrimp, cooked and shredded
¼ cup water chestnuts, sliced
¼ cup mushrooms, sliced
2 tablespoons soy sauce
pinch ground ginger

Heat oil in heavy frying pan or wok. Add onion, and garlic if desired, and stir-fry for 2 or 3 minutes. Meanwhile, steam the wheat sprouts for 10 minutes. Add to frying pan and stir-fry until lightly browned. Add shrimp, bean sprouts, water chestnuts, mushrooms, soy sauce and ginger. Bring to piping hot and serve immediately with a crisp green salad.

Shrimp With Sprouts

(2 to 4 Servings)

2 cups Mung Bean Sprouts
3 tablespoons peanut, safflower or corn oil
1 small onion, sliced thin
1 cup cooked shrimp, diced
½ cup celery, shredded
3 tablespoons parsley, minced
½ cup water chestnuts, sliced
¼ cup mushrooms, sliced

½ cup chicken broth
1 tablespoon cornstarch
2 tablespoons soy sauce
pinch of ginger
pinch of salt

Heat oil in heavy frying pan or wok. Add onion and stir-fry for 2 or 3 minutes. Add shrimp, celery, parsley, water chestnuts and mushrooms. Stir-fry for another 1 or 2 minutes. Add sprouts and stir-fry for 1 or 2 minutes. Meanwhile combine chicken broth, cornstarch, soy sauce, ginger and salt. Add broth mixture to shrimp-sprout mixture in frying pan and bring to bubbling hot. Cook covered until sauce has thickened. Serve immediately over noodles or rice.

Clam and Sprout Sauce

(2 or 3 Servings)

Use this as you would any spaghetti sauce over firm-cooked spaghetti or vermicelli.

2 cups Mung Bean Sprouts
4 tablespoons peanut, safflower or corn oil
½ cup onion, diced
1 garlic clove, minced fine
½ cup cooked mushrooms, sliced
½ cup pimiento, shredded
1 cup clam broth
1 tablespoon cornstarch
2 tablespoons soy sauce
1 teaspoon sugar
salt and pepper to taste
1 cup cooked and minced clams

Heat oil in large heavy frying pan. Add onion and garlic. Cook until onion is translucent. Add sprouts, mushrooms, and pimiento. Stir-fry for 2 or 3 minutes. Mix together clam broth, cornstarch, soy sauce, sugar, salt and pepper. Add to sprout mixture and cook until juice thickens. Add clams and mix well. Bring to bubbling hot very quickly, stirring all the while. Serve over hot spaghetti or vermicelli, with grated cheese if desired.

Eggs Fu Yung

(2 to 4 Servings)

This basic recipe is good as is or as only a beginning. The variations are endless—add any leftover chicken, meat, fish or seafood on hand.

> 1½ cups Mung Bean Sprouts
> 4 large eggs
> ½ cup finely minced onion
> 1 tablespoon diced celery or green pepper
> 1 teaspoon salt
> oil for frying

Beat eggs until frothy. Add sprouts, onion, celery or green pepper and salt. Mix well. Heat 1 tablespoon oil in small (4- or 6-inch size is best) frying pan. Spoon about ¼ cup egg mixture into pan. Cook quickly until brown on one side and turn to cook other side. Remove from pan and drain on paper. Repeat until all egg mixture is used. Keep the patties warm in oven until all are cooked.

Serve with soy sauce or gravy made from 1 cup chicken broth, 1 tablespoon cornstarch, 2 tablespoons soy sauce, salt and pepper to taste. Gravy should be cooked until thick and served hot.

Egg Rolls

(15 to 18 Rolls)

A favorite Chinese food, these egg rolls look complicated, but are really very easy to make. They can be made ahead and frozen or refrigerated until needed, then oven-heated for serving. Any chicken, shrimp, fish or other leftover meats you have on hand can be added to the filling mixture.

> *Wrapping;*
> 2 eggs, well beaten
> 1½ cups water
> 2 cups flour
> ½ teaspoon salt
> oil for frying

Filling:

2 cups Mung Bean Sprouts
1 cup cabbage, shredded fine
1 cup celery, shredded fine
¼ cup diced mushrooms
1 large onion, shredded fine
2 tablespoons soy sauce
2 cups leftover meat, shredded (optional)

For wrapping, combine all ingredients except oil. Heat 6-inch frying pan and grease lightly. Put 1 large spoonful of wrapping mixture in pan. Cook quickly without turning until bottom is brown and top is dry. Remove to plate. Repeat until all wrapping mix is used.

Combine all ingredients for filling in a large bowl. Put about 2 tablespoons of filling mixture on each wrapping. Fold in sides and roll tightly. Deep fry until golden brown.

Seafood Omelet

(2 or 3 Servings)

With one of the quick hot sprout breads and a salad, this is a very satisfying luncheon or light dinner meal.

1 cup Mung Bean Sprouts
4 eggs, well beaten
2 tablespoons finely minced onion
½ teaspoon salt
pinch of pepper
½ cup cooked and shredded shrimp or lobster
2 tablespoons parsley, chopped

Combine sprouts, eggs, onion, salt and pepper. Pour into lightly greased omelet or frying pan. Cook slowly until bottom is brown and top dry. Sprinkle shrimp or lobster on half the omelet. Fold over other half. Serve immediately, garnished with chopped parsley.

Sprout Soufflé

(2 or 3 Servings)

1½ cups Mung Bean Sprouts
4 eggs
2 tablespoons chopped chives
1 tablespoon chopped parsley
½ teaspoon salt
pinch of pepper

Separate eggs. Beat egg yolks until frothy. Add sprouts, chives, parsley, salt and pepper. Mix well. In another bowl, beat egg whites until stiff and dry. Fold into egg yolk mixture. Put in greased 1-quart baking dish. Bake at 350 until puffed and lightly brown on top. Serve immediately with mushroom, tomato or soy sauce.

If desired, this dish may be used to make individual soufflés, using greased custard cups.

Soy Sprouts Alfredo

(2 or 3 Servings)

A quick, nutritious and tasty entrée that goes well with cold sliced meat and salad.

1½ cups Soybean Sprouts
½ cup grated cheese
¼ cup instant dry milk
2 tablespoons melted butter or margarine
salt and pepper to taste

Cook sprouts by steaming for 15 to 20 minutes or by boiling for 8 to 10 minutes. (Sprouts should be cooked enough to get rid of the raw bean taste, but not enough so they are mushy.) Drain sprouts, put in a medium-sized pan and set in a larger pan of boiling water. Sprinkle half the cheese and all the dry milk over sprouts. Toss well. Add melted butter, balance of the cheese, salt and pepper. Toss lightly but thoroughly until cheese melts.

Variation: for added taste appeal, dice and fry 2 or 3 strips of bacon or a small slice of ham, and add to cooked sprouts and cheese mixture.

Cheese and Bean Sprout Soufflé

(2 to 4 Servings)

An excellent luncheon dish. Serve with one of the hot quick sprout breads and a salad.

1 cup Mung Bean Sprouts
2 tablespoons butter or margarine
2 tablespoons flour
½ cup scalded milk
½ teaspoon salt
pinch of pepper
2/3 cup grated cheese
2 tablespoons onion, minced fine
3 egg yolks, well beaten
3 egg whites, beaten stiff and dry

In small pan melt butter or margarine. Add flour and mix well. Add scalded milk gradually, stirring until smooth. Add salt, pepper, grated cheese and onion. Remove from fire and put in medium-sized bowl. Let cool slightly and add egg yolks and sprouts. Blend thoroughly and fold in egg whites. Pour into greased baking dish and bake 20 minutes at 325. Serve immediately.

Wheat Sprout and Cheese Loaf

(4 or 5 Servings)

3 cups Wheat Sprouts, chopped or coarsely ground
2/3 cup soft bread, crumbled and packed down
¼ cup wheat germ
¼ cup minced onion
¼ cup minced celery
2 tablespoons minced green pepper
2 eggs, well beaten
3 tablespoons melted butter or margarine
¾ cup grated or shredded cheese
salt and pepper to taste
milk as needed

Combine all ingredients in mixing bowl. Mix thoroughly, adding a small amount of milk if necessary to make mixture blend well. Put in greased loaf pan. Bake at 350 for 45 to 50 minutes (loaf should be brown on top, but not dry). Serve with tomato sauce, if desired.

Mung Bean Sprouts au Gratin

(2 to 4 Servings)

3 cups Mung Bean Sprouts
2 tablespoons butter or margarine
2 tablespoons flour
1¼ cups scalded milk
1 teaspoon Worcestershire sauce
3 tablespoons onion, finely minced
1 cup cheese, diced or shredded
¼ teaspoon celery salt
½ teaspoon salt
¼ cup bread crumbs

Melt butter in saucepan. Add flour and mix well. Slowly add scalded milk, stirring constantly until mixture thickens. Remove from fire. Add Worcestershire sauce, onion, cheese, celery salt, salt and sprouts. Mix thoroughly and put in greased baking dish. Top with bread crumbs. Bake at 350 for 30 minutes.

Cheese and Wheat Sprout Croquettes

(4 to 6 Servings)

This dish is equally good as an entrée or as an appetizer.

1 cup barely sprouted Wheat Sprouts, coarsely ground
2 tablespoons butter or margarine
2 tablespoons flour
2/3 cup scalded milk
½ teaspoon salt
pinch of pepper

2/3 cup grated cheese
3 tablespoons minced onion
1 egg, beaten lightly
½ cup bread crumbs or wheat germ
beaten egg for dipping croquettes

Melt butter or margarine in small saucepan. Add flour and mix well. Slowly add scalded milk, stirring until smooth. Add salt, pepper, cheese and onion. Remove from fire. Add the lightly beaten egg and sprouts. Let mixture cool somewhat. Form into 1½- to 2-inch croquettes or balls. Dip alternately in bread crumbs or wheat germ, beaten egg and crumbs again. Fry in deep fat and drain on paper. Serve piping hot.

If used as an appetizer, make smaller balls and serve hot on a toothpick.

Variation: for an Oriental touch, serve with mustard or sweet and sour sauce.

Sprout Stuffed Eggplant

(2 Servings)

2 cups sprouts, any kind (Wheat, Mung or Pea Bean,
    Rice, etc.)
1 large eggplant
2 tablespoons peanut, safflower or corn oil
1 small onion, diced
1 stalk celery, diced
1 tablespoon minced parsley
salt and pepper to taste
2 tablespoons grated cheese
2 tablespoons wheat germ

Cut eggplant in half lengthwise. Scoop out center, leaving about ½-inch shell. Put oil in small frying pan. Add onion and sauté until lightly brown. Dice center part of eggplant. Add sautéed onion, celery, parsley, salt and pepper. Mix well and stuff into eggplant shells. Put on greased baking sheet. Top with mixed cheese and wheat germ. Bake at 350 for 45 to 50 minutes. Eggplant should be thoroughly cooked but not mushy. Serve with tomato sauce, if desired.

Sprout Burgers

(2 to 4 Servings)

1 cup barely sprouted Wheat Sprouts
1 cup Adzuki Bean Sprouts
½ cup Soybean Sprouts
½ cup Pea or Lentil Sprouts
1 medium onion
1 egg, well beaten
½ cup milk
2 tablespoons wheat germ
salt and pepper to taste

Grind together the sprouts and onion. Put in bowl. Add egg, milk, wheat germ, salt and pepper. Mix thoroughly, adding more milk if needed. Form into patties and put on lightly greased baking sheet. Broil until brown but not dried out. Serve as you would any burger. If you don't have the exact quantities or kinds of sprouts called for, substitute what you do have in roughly the same quantities.

Vegetarian Sukiyaki

(2 to 4 Servings)

Meat, fish or chicken can be added to this basic dish if desired.

3 cups Mung Bean Sprouts
3 tablespoons corn, safflower or peanut oil
1 large onion, sliced thin
½ cup celery, shredded
½ cup mushrooms, sliced thin
¼ cup water chestnuts, sliced thin
3 or 4 radishes, sliced thin
½ cup bamboo shoots, cut in bite-size lengths
½ cup vegetable stock or bouillon
1 tablespoon cornstarch
2 tablespoons soy sauce
salt and pepper to taste

Heat oil in large frying pan. Sauté onion until translucent. Add sprouts and all other vegetables. Stir-fry for 2 minutes. In a small bowl combine vegetable stock or bouillon, soy sauce, cornstarch, salt and pepper. Add to vegetable mixture and cook until sauce thickens. Serve immediately.

vegetables

Stir-Fried Mung Bean Sprouts

(2 to 4 Servings)

This is the best known use for bean sprouts and the one that most people first think of when you talk about sprouts. No two cooks ever do this dish exactly the same way and the possible variations are legion. Canned Mung Bean Sprouts are widely available, but they do not have the same flavor and crisp texture as fresh ones.

2 cups Mung Bean Sprouts
1 tablespoon peanut, safflower or corn oil
¼ cup onion, scallions or celery, thin-sliced
soy sauce to taste

Heat oil in heavy frying pan or wok. Sauté onion, scallions or celery for 2 or 3 minutes, stirring constantly. Add well-drained sprouts and stir-fry for another 3 minutes. Season to taste with soy sauce or salt and pepper, as desired.

Green Beans and Sprouts

(2 to 4 Servings)

2 cups Mung Bean Sprouts
2/3 cup vegetable stock or chicken broth
2 cups green beans (fresh or frozen)

    1 tablespoon peanut, safflower or corn oil
    2 tablespoons chopped onion
    salt and pepper to taste
    2 strips bacon, fried crisp

Put vegetable stock or chicken broth in saucepan. Add diagonally-cut or French-sliced green beans and cook covered for about 10 minutes. Meanwhile sauté the onion in oil. Add onion, sprouts and seasonings to the now partly cooked green beans. Cook about 5 minutes more. Serve garnished with crumbled crisp bacon.

Green Peppers and Bean Sprouts

(2 to 4 Servings)

    2 cups Mung Bean Sprouts
    3 tablespoons peanut, safflower or corn oil
    3 green peppers
    2 tablespoons chopped onion or scallion
    1 teaspoon salt
    pinch garlic powder

Heat oil in wok or heavy frying pan. Add seeded and thinly sliced green peppers. Saute for 2 or 3 minutes. Add onion and stir-fry for another 1 or 2 minutes. Add sprouts, salt and garlic powder. Cover and cook for 5 minutes.

Sesame Seeded Bean Sprouts

(2 to 4 Servings)

    2 cups Mung Bean Sprouts
    1 tablespoon peanut, safflower or corn oil
    1 small onion or 2 scallions, chopped
    2 tablespoons toasted sesame seeds
    soy sauce or salt and pepper to taste

Heat oil in wok or heavy frying pan. Add onion or scallions and stir-fry for 1 or 2 minutes. Add sprouts, sesame seeds and seasonings. Cook covered for 5 minutes.

Brown Rice and Bean Sprouts

(2 to 4 Servings)

Leftover rice can be used in this recipe which is particularly good with fish or chicken.

1 cup Mung Bean Sprouts
2 tablespoons peanut, safflower or corn oil
1 tablespoon chopped scallion, onion or chives
¼ cup thin-sliced mushrooms (fresh or canned)
1 tablespoon soy sauce
1 cup cooked brown rice

Heat oil in wok or heavy frying pan. Add scallion or onion and mushrooms. Stir-fry until lightly browned. Add soy sauce, rice and sprouts. Stir-fry for 3 or 4 minutes. Cover and simmer for 5 minutes.

Variation idea: omit soy sauce and substitute herbs and seasonings of your own choice—a touch of thyme and rosemary, for example.

Broccoli and Bean Sprouts

(2 to 4 Servings)

1½ cups Mung Bean Sprouts
2 tablespoons peanut, safflower or corn oil
½ cup chopped onion
1 cup chopped broccoli (fresh or frozen)
1 cup snow peas or fresh or frozen garden peas
soy sauce or salt and pepper to taste
pinch of ground ginger
¼ cup toasted almond slivers for garnish

Heat oil in wok or heavy frying pan. Add chopped onion and stir-fry for 1 or 2 minutes. Add each remaining ingredient, stir-frying a few minutes before adding the next. Garnish with almond slivers.

Variation idea: omit the snow peas or peas and substitute thin sliced mushrooms—fresh if possible.

Cabbage and Mung Bean Sprouts

(2 to 4 Servings)

1 cup Mung Bean Sprouts
2 tablespoons peanut, safflower or corn oil
1½ cups shredded cabbage, red is preferred
1 teaspoon vinegar
1 teaspoon soy sauce
salt and pepper to taste

Heat oil in wok or heavy frying pan. Add shredded cabbage—red is particularly eye-appealing—and sauté for 2 or 3 minutes. Add sprouts and stir-fry for another 2 minutes. Sprinkle with seasonings and toss lightly.

Creamed Sprouts

(2 or 3 Servings)

This is a marvelous way to use up that small batch of sprouts that isn't quite big enough to make a dish by itself. Any kind may be used.

1 or 2 cups cooked sprouts
2 tablespoons butter or margarine
2 tablespoons flour
1 cup milk or light cream
salt and pepper to taste
chopped parsley or chives

Melt butter or margarine in top of double boiler or in heavy saucepan. Stir in flour and mix until well blended. Heat milk or cream and add gradually to butter-flour mixture, beating rapidly (a wire whisk is the best utensil to use). Bring mixture to boiling point and then lower heat to simmer. Cook for 5 minutes. Add the precooked sprouts and season to taste. Cook covered for 5 minutes more. Serve garnished with chopped parsley or chives.

Variation idea: add ½ cup grated cheese and a drop or two of Tabasco sauce.

Mushrooms and Sprouts

(2 or 3 Servings)

Try this recipe with different sprouts—the result is never twice the same, but always delicious.

> 1 cup Alfalfa, Cabbage, Clover, Fenugreek, Mustard
>   or Radish Sprouts
> 2 tablespoons peanut, safflower or corn oil
> ½ cup chopped onion
> ½ cup diced celery
> 2/3 cup sliced mushrooms (fresh or canned,
>   though fresh are best)
> soy sauce or salt and pepper to taste
> ¼ cup toasted almond slivers

Heat oil in wok or heavy frying pan. Add onion, celery and mushrooms. Stir-fry for 3 or 4 minutes. Add sprouts and cover. Cook for about 5 minutes—only until sprouts are done but not soggy. Season to taste with soy sauce or salt and pepper. Serve garnished with almonds.

Spinach and Sprouts

(2 to 4 Servings)

> 1½ cups Bean or Pea Sprouts (Mung, Pea, Garbanzo or Lentil)
> 2 tablespoons peanut, safflower or corn oil
> ½ cup sliced mushrooms (fresh or canned)
> ¼ cup meat broth or bouillon
> 1 cup chopped raw spinach (fresh or frozen)
> 1 tablespoon soy sauce or salt and pepper to taste

Heat oil in wok or heavy frying pan. Add mushrooms and stir-fry until brown. Add broth or bouillon and sprouts. Cook covered until sprouts are nearly done—about 5 to 8 minutes, depending on the kind you have used. Add spinach and cook for another 2 or 3 minutes. Season to taste.

Variation idea: sprinkle with finely chopped hard-boiled egg.

Sprouted Rice and Beans

(2 to 4 Servings)

This recipe is particularly good if made with one of the heartier bean sprouts—Black, Pinto, Kidney, Red or Adzuki. Each will give the dish a distinctly different flavor.

1 cup Bean Sprouts
1 cup Rice Sprouts
1 tablespoon peanut, safflower or corn oil
1 small onion, chopped
¼ cup ham or Canadian bacon, diced
¼ cup green pepper, chopped
¼ cup water
½ teaspoon salt
¼ teaspoon pepper

Heat oil in wok or heavy frying pan. Add onion, ham or bacon and green pepper. Sauté for 3 or 4 minutes—until onion is translucent. Add sprouts. water, salt and pepper. Cook covered until sprouts are tender —15 to 30 minutes.

Creole Soy Sprouts

(2 to 4 Servings)

2 cups Soybean Sprouts
2 tablespoons peanut, safflower or corn oil
¼ cup minced onion
1/3 cup diced celery
2 cups cooked tomatoes
½ bay leaf
1 teaspoon salt

Heat oil in a heavy saucepan. Add onion and celery. Sauté until lightly browned. Add tomatoes, bay leaf and salt. Bring to boil and cook slowly for 10 minutes. Remove bay leaf and add sprouts. Cook covered for 15 to 20 minutes—until sprouts are tender.

Variation: substitute Mung, Lentil or Pea Bean sprouts and reduce cooking time to 8 or 10 minutes.

Stir-Fried Soybean Sprouts

(2 to 4 Servings)

Soybean sprouts are rather bland tasting, so the bits of ham add nicely to this dish.

2 cups Soybean Sprouts
1 tablespoon peanut, safflower or corn oil
2 tablespoons chopped scallion, onion or chives
¼ cup shredded ham
¼ cup meat or vegetable stock or water
1 tablepoon soy sauce
pinch of sugar

Heat oil in wok or heavy frying pan. Add scallion, onion or chives and stir-fry for 1 minute. Add ham and stir-fry another minute. Add sprouts, meat or vegetable stock, soy sauce and sugar. Stir-fry for 2 or 3 minutes. Cover tightly and simmer for 20 to 30 minutes—until sprouts are tender.

Celery and Pea Sprouts

(2 to 4 Servings)

2 cups Pea Sprouts
2 tablespoons peanut, safflower or corn oil
8 stalks celery, cut diagonally into 1-inch pieces
salt to taste

Heat oil in heavy frying pan. Add celery and stir-fry for 2 or 3 minutes. Add sprouts and cook covered for about 6 minutes. Salt to taste.

Chickpea Sprouts with Bacon

(2 to 4 Servings)

2 cups Chickpea Sprouts
1 thick slice Canadian bacon, diced
2 tablespoons chopped scallion, onion or chives
1 tablespoon soy sauce

Cook diced bacon in heavy frying pan or wok for 5 minutes. Add chopped scallion, onion or chives. Stir-fry for 2 or 3 minutes. Add sprouts and soy sauce. Cover and cook for about 6 or 7 minutes. Sprouts should be tender but still crisp.

Black-eyed Pea Sprouts

(2 to 4 Servings)

2 cups Black-eyed Pea Sprouts
2 strips bacon, minced
1 small onion, chopped
¼ cup water
½ teaspoon thyme
½ teaspoon salt

Put bacon and onion in heavy frying pan and cook slowly until bacon is done. Add water, sprouts and seasonings. Cook covered for 10 to 12 minutes—until sprouts are done.

Stir-Fried Wheat Sprouts

(2 to 4 Servings)

2 cups Wheat Sprouts
1 tablespoon peanut, safflower or corn oil
2 tablespoons finely chopped onion or scallion
¼ cup sliced water chestnuts
1 tablespoon soy sauce
pinch of ground ginger

Heat oil in wok or heavy frying pan. Add onion or scallion and stir-fry for 1 or 2 minutes. Add sprouts, water chestnuts, soy sauce and ginger. Cook covered for 5 minutes.

Variation: omit ginger and/or soy sauce, substituting herbs of your own choice.

Hash Browned Potatoes and Sprouts

(2 to 4 Servings)

A nice way to use up leftover potatoes. Add some leftover or cold sliced meat and you have a quick and tasty cold-weather lunch.

  1 cup Fenugreek Sprouts
  2 tablespoons peanut, safflower or corn oil
  2 or 3 large cooked potatoes, diced
  1 teaspoon salt
  chopped parsley

Heat oil in wok or heavy frying pan. Add potato and cook until lightly browned. Add sprouts and salt. Cook covered for 5 minutes. Serve garnished with parsley.

Variation: many sprouts are tasty used in this combination. Try your favorite and see if you like it.

breads

Sprouts can be added to almost any bread recipe for extra nutrition. Moisture content will vary between different kinds of sprouts and between batches of the same kind, so you will want to experiment a bit. Try substituting one-half to one cup of chopped fresh or ground dried sprouts for an equivalent amount of flour. Then increase the amount of sprouts in subsequent bakings. If fresh sprouts are used, it will be necessary to decrease the amount of liquid the recipe calls for. Too large a percentage of sprouts will give you soggy bread, so don't use more than half sprouts at most in any recipe.

The following quick breads are easy to make and tasty.

Alfalfa Muffins

(10 to 12 Muffins)

    1 cup barely sprouted Alfalfa Sprouts
    1 cup whole wheat flour
    1 cup white flour
    3 teaspoons baking powder
    ½ teaspoon salt
    1 egg, well beaten
    1 tablespoon honey or molasses
    1 cup milk
    3 tablespoons melted shortening

Sift flours, baking powder and salt together. Add egg, honey or molasses, milk and sprouts. Mix well and add melted shortening. Bake in well-greased muffin pans at 375 for 25 or 30 minutes.

Corn Meal and Sprout Muffins

(10 to 12 Muffins)

These muffins are particularly good with *Green Pea Sprout Soup* or *Beef and Lentil Soup* for a nice luncheon touch.

    ½ cup oven-dried Wheat or Rice Sprouts
    ½ cup corn meal
    1 cup white flour
    4 teaspoons baking powder
    ½ teaspoon salt
    1 tablespoon sugar
    1 cup milk or water
    1 egg, well beaten
    3 tablespoons melted shortening

Sift corn meal, flour, baking powder, salt and sugar together. Add milk or water and egg. Mix thoroughly. Add sprouts and melted shortening. Bake in well-greased muffin pans at 400 for 20 minutes.

Rice Sprout Muffins

(12 Medium Muffins)

¾ cup partly cooked Rice Sprouts
2¼ cups white flour
5 teaspoons baking powder
1 tablespoon sugar or honey
½ teaspoon salt
1 cup milk or water
1 egg, well beaten
2 tablespoons melted shortening

Sift flour, baking powder, sugar (if honey is used, add with the liquids), and salt together. Add milk or water and egg. Mix thoroughly. Add the sprouts and melted shortening. Bake in well-greased muffin pans at 400 for 20 minutes.

Variation: add finely chopped dates or figs to the dough and omit the sweetening.

Sprout and Bran Muffins

(10 to 12 Muffins)

These are hearty muffins—equally good for a cold-weather lunch or breakfast.

1 cup oven-dried Wheat Sprouts, ground
1 cup whole wheat or graham flour
1 tablespoon sugar
¼ teaspoon salt
1½ teaspoons soda
½ cup bran (or wheat germ)
1¼ cups sour milk or yogurt
1 egg, well beaten
2 tablespoons melted shortening

Sift flour, sugar, salt and soda together. Add sprouts and bran, mixing well. Add sour milk or yogurt and egg. Mix thoroughly and add melted shortening. Bake in well-greased muffin pans at 350 for 25 minutes.

Wheat Sprout Biscuits

(20 Small or 12 Large Biscuits)

Quick and easy to make, these biscuits make a good accompaniment to a soup and salad lunch.

   1 cup oven-dried Wheat Sprouts, ground
   1 cup white flour
   5 teaspoons baking powder
   ½ teaspoon salt
   2 tablespoons shortening
   1 cup milk or water

Sift flour, baking powder and salt together. Add the sprouts. Cut in shortening with pastry cutter or knife. Add milk or water. Put dough on floured board and pat out to ½-inch thickness. Cut with biscuit cutter and place on greased baking sheet. Bake at 450 for about 15 minutes.

Rye Sprout Crisps

(30 to 40 Crackers)

These crisp crackers, with their nut-like flavor, can be used with almost any dip or spread for snacks.

   2 cups oven-dried Rye Sprouts, ground
   1 cup flour (part white and part rye)
   ½ teaspoon salt
   2 tablespoons melted butter
   1 egg, well beaten

Mix sprouts, flour and salt. Add melted butter and egg. Mix well. If dough is too stiff, add a few drops of water; if too wet, add a little more white flour. Knead on a floured board until dough is smooth and firm. Roll dough out very thin (about 1/8 inch) and cut into small square, triangular and circular cracker shapes. Prick each piece in several places and bake on a well-greased cookie sheet at 400 for 10 minutes.

   Variation idea: omit salt in dough and sprinkle sea salt on crackers before baking, or sprinkle with caraway seeds or poppy seeds.

Unleavened Wheat Sticks

(12 to 18 Sticks)

Easy to make, highly nutritious and very tasty.

    4 cups barely sprouted Wheat Sprouts
    ½ teaspoon salt
    1 egg
    ½ cup corn meal or sesame seeds

Towel dry the sprouts and grind very fine in food grinder or blender. Add salt and beaten egg. Mix thoroughly. Shape into sticks 6 or 8 inches long and about ½ inch in diameter. Roll in corn meal and place on greased baking sheet. Leave to dry while oven reaches 400. Bake 10 minutes and lower temperature to 325 and bake for about 5 minutes more.

The following yeast breads are excellent—and wholesome.

Sprouted Wheat Bread

(2 Loaves)

    2 cups Wheat Sprouts
    3 cups warm water
    2 cakes yeast (or 2 envelopes dry)
    ¼ cup honey or molasses
    3 tablespoons cooking oil
    1 tablespoon salt
    5 to 6 cups whole wheat flour

Dissolve yeast in part of the water. Add remaining water, honey or molasses, cooking oil and salt. Mix well and gradually add 3 cups flour. Beat until light and elastic. Let dough rise until double in bulk—about 1 hour. Meanwhile, dry sprouts between layers of paper towel to remove as much moisture as possible. Grind dried sprouts in food grinder or blender. Add ground sprouts and remaining flour to dough and beat until mixture can be kneaded.

Knead for 8 to 10 minutes on floured board until dough is smooth and stretchy. Place in an oiled bowl and cover with damp cloth. Let rise in a warm place until double in bulk. Punch dough down and divide into two oiled 9 x 5-inch pans. Let rise again until double in bulk—about 30 minutes. Bake about 1 hour at 350. Remove from pans and cool on rack.

Experiment with this recipe, using warm milk instead of water and by varying the ratio of sprouts to flour—it's delicious every way.

Whole-Sprout Wheat Bread

(2 Loaves)

The addition of some whole sprouts gives this bread an interesting and different texture.

    1 cup Wheat Sprouts, left whole
    1 cup Wheat Sprouts, ground
    3 cups warm water
    2 cakes yeast (or 2 envelopes dry)
    ¼ cup honey or corn syrup
    3 tablespoons cooking oil
    1 tablespoon salt
    2 cups whole wheat flour
    3 to 4 cups white flour

Dissolve yeast in part of the water. Add remaining water, honey or corn syrup, cooking oil and salt. Stir well. Add the whole wheat flour and 2½ to 3 cups of the white flour. Beat well. Cover and put dough in a warm place to double in bulk—about 1 hour. While the dough is rising, prepare the ground sprouts by patting dry between paper towels and grinding in a food grinder or blender. Add the ground and whole sprouts to the risen dough, adding more white flour if necessary. Knead until elastic and smooth. Put dough in an oiled bowl, cover and let rise in a warm place until double in bulk. Punch down and form into two loaves. Place in oiled 9 x 5-inch pans and let rise again until double in bulk—about ½ hour this time. Bake in a 350 oven for 1 to 1½ hours. Remove from pans and cool on rack.

Sprouted White Bread

(2 Loaves)

1 cup Wheat or Rye Sprouts
1 cake yeast (or 1 envelope dry)
1 cup warm water
1¼ cups milk
2 tablespoons butter
1 tablespoon sugar
2 teaspoons salt
6 to 7 cups white flour

Dissolve yeast in warm water. Scald milk and remove from stove. Add butter, sugar and salt. Stir well and let cool to lukewarm. Combine with yeast mixture. Add 6 cups white flour and beat thoroughly. Place dough in oiled bowl, cover and put in warm place to rise until double in bulk. Punch down dough and turn out on a floured board. Sprinkle towel-dried sprouts over the dough and knead until sprouts are evenly distributed. Divide dough between 2 oiled 9 x 5-inch pans. Let rise again until double in bulk. Preheat oven to 400 and bake for 10 minutes. Reduce heat to 350 and bake for about 30 minutes more—until loaves sound hollow and have pulled away from the edges of the pans. Remove from pans and cool on rack.

Sprouted Alfalfa Bread

(2 Loaves)

3 cups Alfalfa Sprouts
1 medium potato with skin
3½ cups warm water
2 cakes yeast (or 2 envelopes dry)
½ cup honey or corn syrup
3 tablespoons cooking oil
2 teaspoons salt
8 or 9 cups flour (part white, part whole wheat)

Dice potato and cook in 3 cups water until tender. Blend potato and water in blender until smooth. Strain to remove particles of potato skin. Dissolve yeast in ½ cup warm water. Add honey or corn syrup, salt, cooking oil and potato liquid. Mix thoroughly. Add towel-dried sprouts and about 5 cups of flour. Knead well, adding additional flour as needed to make dough smooth and elastic. Place in oiled bowl, cover and let rise in a warm place until double in bulk. Punch dough down and form into 2 loaves. Place in 2 oiled 9 x 5-inch pans and let rise again until double in bulk. Bake in 350 oven for 1 to 1¼ hours, until well done and golden brown on top. Remove from pans and cool on rack.

Sprouted Bread Sticks

(2 Dozen Sticks)

These bread sticks go with soup and make fine after-school snacks.

1 cup Wheat Sprouts
¾ cup warm water
1 cake yeast (or 1 envelope dry)
1 tablespoon honey
2 tablespoons butter
1 teaspoon salt
2 cups flour (part white and part whole wheat)
1 egg
sesame or poppy seeds

Dissolve yeast in warm water. Add honey, butter, salt, 1 cup flour and the sprouts that have been towel-dried and ground. Beat thoroughly and add rest of the flour. On floured board, knead until smooth. Place in oiled bowl and let rise in a warm place until double in bulk. Punch down dough and cut into 24 equal pieces. Roll each piece into sticks 8 inches long. Arrange on greased cookie sheet about 1 inch apart. Brush with well-beaten egg and sprinkle with sesame or poppy seeds. Bake in a preheated 375 oven for 15 to 20 minutes—until golden brown.

Refrigerator Sprout Rolls

(2 Dozen Small Rolls)

These are nice, light rolls that go equally well with dinner or a soup and salad lunch.

1 cup Wheat or Rye Sprouts
1½ cups milk
1 cake yeast (or 1 envelope dry)
3 tablespoons shortening
3 tablespoons sugar
1 teaspoon salt
1 egg
3 to 4 cups white flour

Scald milk and let cool. Dissolve yeast in milk. Add shortening, sugar and salt. Add well-beaten egg and 3 cups flour. Beat rapidly for 2 or 3 minutes. Add sprouts that have been towel-dried. On floured board, knead until dough is smooth and elastic, adding more flour if necessary. Place in an oiled bowl in refrigerator for at least 4 hours. 2 hours before mealtime, remove dough from refrigerator and shape into rolls. Let rise until dough has doubled—about 30 to 40 minutes. Bake in 400 oven for about 15 minutes—until rolls are golden brown.

sweet things

Sprout Spice Cake

(One 8-inch Cake)

A nice, moist spice cake that keeps well.

> ½ cup oven-dried Soy Sprouts, toasted
> 2 cups sifted cake flour
> 2 teaspoons baking powder
> ¾ cup sugar
> ½ teaspoon salt
> ½ teaspoon cinnamon
> ½ teaspoon nutmeg
> ¼ teaspoon cloves
> 5 tablespoons shortening
> ½ cup molasses
> 2 eggs, well beaten
> ½ cup milk
> ¾ cup chopped raisins or whole currants
> ¾ cup favorite white frosting

Sift together flour, baking powder, sugar, salt and spices. Add shortening and molasses. Blend well. Combine eggs and milk. Add to flour-shortening mixture, stirring until just blended. Add sprouts and raisins or currants. Beat vigorously for 1 minute. Pour into greased 8-inch square pan. Bake at 375 for 35 minutes. Let cool and spread with white frosting. Or, if you prefer, leave plain or sprinkle with confectioner's sugar.

Variation: you can do almost anything with this fine spice cake. Try other oven-dried and toasted sprouts that you may have on hand.

Wheat Sprout and Oatmeal Cookies

(About 3 Dozen Cookies)

1½ cups oven-dried Wheat Sprouts, coarsely ground
¾ cup liquid shortening
¾ cup brown sugar
2 eggs, well beaten
¼ cup milk
1½ cups uncooked oatmeal
½ cup flour
1 teaspoon baking powder
1 teaspoon salt
½ teaspoon cinnamon
½ teaspoon allspice

Cream shortening and sugar. Add eggs, milk and oatmeal. Mix and sift together flour, baking powder, salt and spices. Drop by teaspoon on greased cookie sheet. Bake at 350 for about 15 minutes—until golden brown.

Almond-Sprout Cookies

(About 3 Dozen Cookies)

2 cups oven-dried Soy Sprouts, finely ground
½ cup shortening
1¼ cups sugar
2 eggs, well beaten
¼ cup milk
1 teaspoon almond flavoring
2 cups flour
1 tablespoon baking powder
½ teaspoon salt

Cream shortening and sugar together. Add eggs, milk and almond flavoring. Sift together flour, baking powder and salt. Add to first mixture. Mix well. Drop by teaspoonsful on greased baking sheet. Bake at 350 for 20 to 25 minutes, until lightly browned.

Soy Sprout Cookies

(About 3 Dozen Cookies)

1¾ cups oven-dried Soy Sprouts, coarsely ground
1/3 cup shortening or margarine
2/3 cup brown sugar
1 egg, well beaten
5 tablespoons milk
½ cup chopped raisins
½ cup chopped nuts
1½ cups white flour
½ teaspoon salt
½ teaspoon baking soda
½ teaspoon cinnamon
½ teaspoon clove
½ teaspoon allspice

Cream shortening or margarine and sugar together. Add egg and milk. Mix well. Add sprouts, raisins and nuts. Mix thoroughly. Mix and sift flour, salt, soda and spices together. Add to the first mixture and mix thoroughly. Drop from teaspoon on greased baking sheet, leaving about 1 inch between cookies. Bake at 325 for 15 minutes—or until golden brown.

Date-Sprout Chews

(2 Dozen Pieces)

1 cup oven-dried Soy Sprouts, toasted
1 cup stoned dates
½ cup coconut
2 teaspoons cream or condensed milk
3 teaspoons vanilla
½ cup brown sugar
¼ cup confectioner's sugar

Put sprouts, dates and coconut through medium blade of food grinder. Add cream or condensed milk and vanilla. Blend thoroughly. Form mixture into small, firm balls. Roll first in brown sugar and then confectioner's sugar.

Sprout Fudge Squares

(16 Squares)

1 cup oven-dried Soy Sprouts, toasted
½ cup shortening
1½ cups sugar
2 eggs
2 (1-oz.) squares unsweetened chocolate, melted
1 teaspoon vanilla
½ cup sifted flour

Cream shortening and sugar together until fluffy. Add eggs one at a time, beating well after each addition. Add chocolate and vanilla and blend well. Add flour and sprouts. Mix well. Pour into greased 8-inch square pan. Bake at 350 for 25 minutes. Let cool in pan. Cut into 2-inch squares.

Sprout Fudge

(25 Pieces)

1 cup oven-dried Soy Sprouts, toasted and chopped coarsely
2/3 cup scalded milk
2 (1-oz.) squares unsweetened chocolate
2 cups sugar
1/8 teaspoon cream of tartar
2 tablespoons butter or margarine
1 teaspoon vanilla

Break chocolate into pieces and melt in scalded milk. Stir until blended. Add sugar and cream of tartar. Cook slowly until sugar is completely dissolved. Bring to boil and cook covered 3 minutes. Uncover and continue cooking until soft-ball stage (236 to 238 on candy thermometer or until soft ball is formed when mixture is dropped in cold water). Stir enough to keep from sticking. Remove from heat and add butter or margarine. Cool to lukewarm without stirring. Add vanilla and beat vigorously until candy is thick. Add sprouts and mix well. Pour into greased 8-inch square pan. When cool, cut into 1½-inch squares.

Peanut Butter-Sprout Fudge

(25 Squares)

½ cup oven-dried Soy Sprouts, chopped coarsely
2 cups sugar
2/3 cup milk
4 tablespoons peanut butter
1 teaspoon vanilla
pinch of salt

Combine sugar and milk in saucepan. Bring to boiling point and cook until a soft ball is formed when mixture is dropped in cold water. Remove from stove. Add peanut butter, vanilla and salt. Beat until creamy. Add sprouts and mix well. Pour into buttered 8-inch square pan. Cool slightly and mark into squares with sharp, pointed knife.

beverages

Soy Sprout Milk No. 1

(1 Quart)

This is a modification of the basic technique for making the soy milk from unsprouted beans that has become such an important part of childrens' diets wherever cow milk is not readily available. As a beverage, this milk is equally palatable and even more nutritious. Unsweetened, it can be used in any recipe that you would ordinarily make with cow milk or light cream.

1½ cups barely sprouted Soybean Sprouts
4 cups warm water
honey or sugar to taste

Blend sprouts and 2 cups water in blender for 5 minutes. Add remaining 2 cups water. Cook in a saucepan over low heat, stirring constantly, for

15 minutes, or in a double boiler over boiling water for 30 minutes. (Soybeans must be thoroughly cooked to be digestible, so don't skimp on the cooking.) When cooked, strain and cool. Keep the resulting soy milk refrigerated. Use the strainer residue in soup, meatloaf, main dishes or gravies.

If the milk is to be served as a beverage, a dash of cinnamon or a few drops of vanilla—in addition to the sweetening—will enhance the flavor. For added nutrition, beat a whole egg into each glass of milk.

Soy Sprout Milk No. 2

(1 Quart)

A quick and easy method to follow if you don't have a blender.

> 1½ cups barely sprouted Soybean Sprouts
> 4 cups water
> honey or sugar to taste

Cook sprouts in water for 15 to 20 minutes. Put through food mill and return to pan. Cook for 5 to 10 minutes more. Force through sieve. Sweeten to taste and follow remainder of instructions for *Soy Sprout Milk No. 1*

Alfalfa Sprout Cocktail

(Two 8-ounce Servings)

> 1 cup Alfalfa Sprouts
> 1½ cups pineapple juice
> 1 very ripe banana
> honey or sugar to taste
> pinch of salt

Blend all ingredients in blender at highest speed for 2 to 3 minutes. (If no blender is available, put sprouts and banana through food mill before adding other ingredients.) Chill thoroughly before serving.

Variation: try adding 2 or 3 tablespoons of undiluted frozen orange juice.

Green Sprout Drink

(Two 8-ounce Servings)

1 cup Mung Bean Sprouts
1 cup Alfalfa Sprouts
½ cup raw spinach, chopped
2 stalks celery, chopped
2 carrots, chopped
2 tablespoons chopped parsley
salt to taste
2 or 3 drops Worcestershire sauce

Put all ingredients in blender and blend at highest speed for 2 or 3 minutes—or until all vegetables have liquified. Serve ice cold.

Tomato and Bean Sprout Drink

(1 Quart)

2 cups Mung Bean Sprouts
3 cups tomato juice or chopped fresh tomatoes
2 stalks celery, chopped
½ green pepper, chopped
1 small onion, chopped
2 tablespoons chopped parsley
salt and pepper to taste

Put all ingredients in blender and blend for 3 or 4 minutes until all vegetables have liquified, or put through food mill and beat with egg beater until frothy. Serve ice cold just as you would tomato juice.

breakfast dishes

Sprout and Fruit Bowl No. 1

(2 or 3 Servings)

1 cup Wheat or Rye Sprouts
1 apple, sliced or grated
1 banana, sliced thin
¼ cup raisins or currants
honey or brown sugar to taste
milk or light cream

Put sprouts in individual serving bowls, cover with sliced or grated apple and sliced banana. Top with raisins or currants. Serve with milk or light cream and honey or brown sugar, if desired.

Variation ideas: add hulled sunflower seeds or substitute yogurt for the milk.

Sprout and Fruit Bowl No. 2

(2 or 3 Servings)

1 cup Wheat Sprouts
1 slice fresh or canned pineapple, cubed
¼ cup raisins or currants
4 tablespoons wheat germ
2 tablespoons sesame seeds
milk or light cream

Put sprouts in individual bowls, add cubed pineapple and raisins or currants. Top with wheat germ and sesame seeds. Serve with milk or light cream.

Variation: substitute apple juice or other fruit juice for the milk or cream.

Dried Wheat Sprout Cereal

(2 or 3 Servings)

    1¼ cups oven-dried Wheat Sprouts
    ½ cup chopped dates, figs or whole raisins
    honey, brown sugar or maple syrup to taste
    milk or light cream

Coarse-grind the sprouts in a food grinder or blender. Divide between individual bowls and top with dried fruit. Serve with choice of sweetening and milk or cream.

Hot Cooked Sprout Cereal

(2 or 3 Servings)

    ½ cup oven-dried Wheat, Rye or Alfalfa Sprouts
    ½ cup cereal oatmeal, cream of wheat or cream of rice
    1 teaspoon butter or margarine
    salt to taste

Combine sprouts with the cereal, salt and butter in Teflon saucepan or double boiler. Cook according to the directions for the cereal, using 50 percent more water than the directions stipulate. Serve with honey, brown sugar or maple syrup and milk or light cream.

    Variation idea: add chopped dried fruit, raisins or currants to the sprouts and cereal before cooking, using a speck more water.

Hot Rice Sprout Cereal

(2 or 3 Servings)

Children particularly like the rich, nutty taste of this cereal.

    1 cup Rice Sprouts
    ½ cup milk
    ¼ cup raisins or other chopped dried fruit
    pinch of salt
    1 teaspoon butter or margarine

Combine all ingredients in Teflon saucepan or double boiler. Cook covered until done—about 30 minutes. Serve with honey or maple syrup for sweetening, and milk or light cream.

Wheat Sprout Waffles

(2 or 3 Large Waffles)

¾ cup ground, oven-dried Wheat Sprouts
1 cup flour
½ teaspoon salt
1 tablespoon baking powder
2 eggs
2 tablespoons sugar
1 cup milk
3 tablespoons corn oil or melted shortening

Sift flour, salt and baking powder into large mixing bowl. In a smaller bowl, beat eggs until frothy and add sugar; combine with flour mixture. Add milk, liquid shortening and sprouts. Cook in a preheated, lightly greased waffle iron until crisp. Serve with honey, maple syrup or softened fruit jam.

Rice Sprout Pancakes

(4 Large or 6 Small Cakes)

1 cup Rice Sprouts
1 cup flour
2 teaspoons baking powder
½ teaspoon salt
1 egg
1 cup milk
2 tablespoons sugar
2 tablespoons corn oil or melted shortening

Sift the flour, baking powder and salt into a large mixing bowl. Beat egg and add to flour mixture. Add milk, sugar, shortening and sprouts. Cook immediately on a preheated, lightly greased griddle or heavy frying pan. Serve with honey, maple syrup or fruit syrup.

Whole Wheat Sprout Pancakes

(4 Large or 6 Small Cakes)

This is good, hearty fare for robust appetites.

1 cup Wheat Sprouts
1 cup whole wheat flour
2 teaspoons baking powder
½ teaspoon salt
2 eggs
2 tablespoons sugar
1 cup milk
3 tablespoons corn oil or melted shortening

Sift flour, baking powder and salt into large mixing bowl. In smaller bowl, beat eggs until frothy and add sugar. Combine egg mixture with flour mixture. Add milk, liquid shortening and wheat sprouts. Cook immediately on a preheated, lightly greased griddle or large, heavy frying pan. Serve with a choice of honey, maple syrup, fruit syrup or softened fruit jam.

Scrambled Eggs With Bean Sprouts

(2 or 3 Servings)

With the addition of a salad and hot bread, this makes an excellent luncheon dish.

½ cup Mung Bean Sprouts
4 eggs
2 tablespoons water
½ teaspoon salt

Beat eggs, water and salt until well blended. Add sprouts. Put mixture in a medium-size, preheated and greased frying pan. Cook over low heat, stirring frequently until done.

Variations: add small, finely chopped onion or 2 tablespoons chopped chives before cooking; or try with Rice Sprouts.

Sprout Omelet

(2 or 3 Servings)

Served with a salad and hot bread, this makes another good luncheon dish.

1 cup Mung Bean or Wheat Sprouts
2 tablespoons butter or cooking oil
4 eggs
2 tablespoons water
½ teaspoon salt
pepper to taste
1 tablespoon chopped parsley

Sauté sprouts in butter in a heavy pan for 2 or 3 minutes. Remove sprouts, keeping the pan warm. Combine eggs, water, salt and pepper in a mixing bowl, beating until frothy. Pour egg mixture into the sautéing pan. Cook over low heat without stirring until eggs have set. Sprinkle with sautéed sprouts and parsley. Fold over the omelet and turn onto a warm platter or serve on individual plates.

Variation idea: substitute soy sauce to taste for the salt and add 2 chopped scallions or 2 tablespoons chopped chives to the egg mixture before cooking.

baby foods

Sprouts are excellent food for babies and young children. As soon as the doctor says the child can have solid food, the following sprout-based dishes may be substituted for comparable store-bought strained baby foods. They will give the baby greater nutrition, without chemical additives or preservatives and at less expense, and they taste good too.

Each of the following recipes makes enough for several baby meals. To have a variety on hand at all times, it is a good idea to make the quantity specified or perhaps even double the recipe and then freeze the results in ice-cube trays. It is, of course, necessary to be sure the trays have been thoroughly sterilized in scalding hot water. After the food is initially frozen, remove the cubes from the trays and store in freezer in tightly closed conventional-style freezer bags.

When it is feeding time, take out one or more cubes (of different kinds) and heat individually in custard cups set in hot water or in one of the small multiple egg poachers, now available.

Mung Bean Sprouts and Egg

(1 Serving)

This is so quick to prepare that it should be made fresh for each feeding.

½ cup Mung Bean Sprouts
1 raw egg yolk
tiny pinch salt

Cook sprouts in the smallest available saucepan with just a trace of water for 3 to 5 minutes, or steam in a covered strainer over boiling water for 8 to 10 minutes. Force through strainer, add egg yolk and salt, and mix well. This may be fed to baby as a change from cereal and egg.

Rice Sprouts and Chicken

(Four 4-ounce Servings)

1½ cups barely sprouted Rice Sprouts
½ to ¾ cup cooked chicken, diced
½ cup chicken broth
¼ teaspoon salt

Put all ingredients in small saucepan. Cook tightly covered, stirring occasionally, for about 30 minutes. Rice should be completely cooked. Add more broth if needed to keep mixture from sticking. When cooked, put mixture through food mill or blend in blender until smooth. Freeze according to general instructions at beginning of this section.

Soybean Sprouts and Liver

(Four 4-ounce Servings)

Soybean Sprouts are particularly high in food value, but they are bland tasting. So only enough liver is used in this dish to make it tasty. If starting with raw liver, it should be broiled slightly before using.

> 2 cups Soybean Sprouts
> 1/3 cup cooked beef liver, diced
> ½ cup beef broth
> ¼ teaspoon salt

Put all ingredients in small saucepan. Cook tightly covered for 30 to 40 minutes, until sprouts are tender. More broth can be added if the liquid cooks away. When cooked, put mixture through food mill or blend in blender until smooth. If not smooth enough, force through strainer. Freeze according to the general instructions at the beginning of this section.

Wheat Sprouts and Meat

(Four 4-ounce Servings)

Any leftover very lean meat—beef, lamb or veal—may be used in this dish, or you can start with uncooked meat. If the latter is used, the meat should be broiled enough to set the juices.

> 1½ cups Wheat Sprouts
> ½ to ¾ cup cooked meat
> ½ cup beef or chicken broth
> ¼ teaspoon salt

Put all ingredients in small saucepan. Cook tightly covered, stirring from time to time, for 30 to 40 minutes. Wheat should be very tender. More broth may be added if needed to keep mixture from sticking to pan. When cooked, put mixture through food mill or blend in blender until smooth. Freeze according to the general directions at the beginning of this section.

Lentil Sprouts and Ham

(Four 4-ounce Servings)

Be sure that every bit of fat is removed from the cooked ham for this recipe.

>2 cups Lentil Sprouts
>1/3 cup cooked ham, diced
>½ cup meat broth or water

Combine all ingredients in small saucepan. Cook tightly covered for 30 to 40 minutes, stirring occasionally. A little more liquid may be added if needed to keep mixture from sticking. When cooked, put mixture through food mill or blend in blender until smooth. The milled or blended mixture may also be forced through a strainer to ensure completely smooth results. Freeze according to general instructions at the beginning of this section.

Quick Sprout Cereal

(Sixteen 2-ounce Servings)

This cereal is highly nutritious and can be used in place of commercial "instant" baby cereals.

>2 cups barely sprouted Wheat Sprouts
>2 cups barely sprouted Rice Sprouts

Put Wheat Sprouts and Rice Sprouts on separate cookie sheets. Roast in 300 oven for 30 to 40 minutes, stirring from time to time. Sprouts must be thoroughly dried out and toasted lightly. (If humidity is high, it may be necessary to leave the oven door open a bit and increase the roasting time.) When thoroughly dry, grind in food grinder or blender until very fine—the consistency of whole wheat flour. Store in tightly closed containers in a cool place—the refrigerator is fine, if the weather is at all warm. Prepare for feeding as with any of the packaged pre-cooked cereals.

Soy Sprout and Fruit Dessert

(Six 4-ounce Servings)

2 cups Soybean Sprouts
½ cup water
1 cup cooked, unsweetened fruit—apple, peach,
    pineapple or pear
lemon juice to taste (optional)
honey or sugar to taste

Combine sprouts and water in saucepan. Cook for 30 minutes. Add fruit and cook for another 1 or 2 minutes (or longer if the fruit is quite firm). Force through food mill or blend in blender until smooth. In the case of rather bland fruits, a few drops of lemon juice will improve flavor. Sweeten to taste, remembering that most doctors recommend that refined sugar be limited in a baby's diet. Freeze according to the directions at the beginning of this section.

Suppliers

In many towns and cities there are health food stores that sell untreated seeds especially for use in sprouting. These stores also often sell various sprouting equipment. However, for those who do not have access to such stores or who prefer to order by mail, the following partial list of suppliers represents at least a few of the many that deal in untreated, edible seeds and/or sprouting equipment. To find out exactly what's available from whom and for how much, write for their price lists and catalogs. Those marked * sell seeds and equipment; those marked † sell seeds only.

*Better Foods Foundation, Inc.
  300 North Washington Street
  Greencastle, Pennsylvania
  17225

*Bio-organic, Inc.
  61 Bruckner Boulevard
  Bronx, New York
  10454

†Boatman's Nursery & Seed Co.
  South Maple Street
  Bainbridge, Ohio
  45612

*Brownie's Natural Foods
  21 East 16th Street
  New York, New York
  10003

†D. V. Burrell Seed Growers Co.
  P. O. Box 150
  Rocky Ford, Colorado
  81067

*Colonial Garden Kitchens
  270 West Merrick Road
  Valley Stream, New York
  11582

*Gary Davis
  736 East 650 South Street
  Centerville, Utah
  84014

*Druff
  2022 Ruth Street
  San Luis Obispo, California
  93401

*Eddie's Sprout Kitchen
  2828 Wainwright Road
  Salt Lake City, Utah
  84109

*Good Earth Natural Foods, Inc.
  1336 First Avenue
  New York, New York
  10021

*Gurney Seed and Nursery Co.
Second and Capital Streets
Yankton, South Dakota
57078

†Charles C. Hart Seed Co.
304 Main Street
Wethersfield, Connecticut
06109

†J. W. Jung Seed Co.
Randolph, Wisconsin
53956

†Kelly Brothers
308 Maple Street
Dansville, New York
14437

†Mellinger's, Inc.
2310 West South Range Road
North Lima, Ohio
44452

†Natural Development Co.
Bainbridge, Pennsylvania
17502

†L. L. Olds Seed Co.
2901 Packers Avenue
P. O. Box 1069
Madison, Wisconsin
53701

*Organic Farm and Garden Center
Box 2806
San Rafael, California
94901

†L. J. Rench & Co.
P. O. Box 211
Dover, Delaware
19901

*Clyde Robin Seed Co.
Box 2091
Castro Valley, California
94546

*Frederic B. Sadtler, Inc.
P. O. Box 323
Fort Washington, Pennsylvania
19034

*Shiloh Farms
Route 59
Sulphur Springs, Arkansas
72768

†Stern's Nurseries, Inc.
Geneva, New York
14456

†Stokes Seeds, Inc.
737 Main Street (Box 548)
Buffalo, New York
14240

*Thompson and Morgan
Box 100
Farmingdale, New Jersey
07727

*Walnut Acres
Natural Foods-Natural Farming
Penns Creek, Pennsylvania
17862

Index